Introduction

I pretty much despise reading. Always have. I own exactly four books – one-time reads. A lil' business and motivation, with some Fifty Shades of Grey sprinkled in. You'll find them tucked neatly away in my nightstand…dust-free and right-aligned, of course.

The role of my Bible is merely a lock box - a convenient camouflage for my handgun and ammo. Yes, I was a true 80s baby, learning all too well from the eerie voice of the *Unsolved Mysteries* narrator that you can never be too cautious, even in a quaint beachside town.

But I digress.

Where was I?

Oh right, I was illustrating my ironic aversion to the written word...

It's not just reading that I avoid. I've never been a fan of writing either. Although my parents raised a model student, performing well above average in almost every academic course, I'm quite impatient. I'm the epitome of high energy. Frankly, I prefer to blurt my thoughts as they come - at warp speed, rather than take the time to write them down. And God forbid I be inconvenienced with adhering to proper punctuation and grammar. Who the hell has time for that?!

But I can't ignore the fact that after only 34 years on this earth, I feel as though I'm bursting with experience and a sort of wisdom that unfortunately seems to come only after uneven rations of joy and heartache. So here we are. I've taken the advice of great friends encouraging me to transcribe my thoughts as they come.

Chelsea's response when I casually tossed out the idea of writing this motivational memoir: "Yes! You're great at showing the importance of positivity, motivation and how attitude makes all the difference. I literally think about your way of life almost every day for inspiration, and I'm not bullshitting you! I envy your will power."

I'm not sure I'm as inspiring as Chelsea makes me seem, but I do think I have a story worth sharing. So here goes nothing. My literacy strike of over a decade has officially come to an end, folks.

"In order to love who you are, you cannot hate the experiences that shaped you."

–Andrea Dykstra

Prologue

My brother Bobby got a tattoo on his chest a few months before he passed away. I'm not sure if it was planned, considering his previously acquired body art was an impulse purchase - the word "WOMP" carved into the inside of his bottom lip.

What does that word even mean? *The Urban Dictionary* tells me it can be "an exclamation used during times in which a plausible response is non-existent." Another (in this case, more likely) definition is "a word used to describe the sound made by the low bass frequencies in dub-step songs." Bobby, without a doubt, functioned on his own unique frequency. He "womped" to the beat of his own drum and did nothing short of shock me with each new endeavor.

A typical conversation with my brother: "Oh hey, by the way, I'll be living on a farm this summer with no electricity or toilet in my cabin," followed by an eager exclamation at how awesome it will be to harvest his own crops…and an offer to gladly cook me an amazing dinner in the near future – one pulled right from the ground. He loved to share his old soul with anyone and everyone. I believe that was his way of spreading love in a world governed by material things.

I think it goes without saying that when Bobby got his second tattoo, he didn't go for the typical bicep armband or Celtic cross like so many college-aged boys at the time. He didn't even get a musical image or marijuana leaf, both of which I assume were top contenders.

Bobby's tattoo was a colorful depiction of a water droplet, bordered by the phrase "Amor Fati." For those of you who don't speak Latin, this translates to "love of one's fate," and is generally used to express the perpetual acceptance of one's life events and circumstances.

I think that for Bobby, these words signified not just accepting, but respecting, loving and truly owning a sense of contentment with his life and who he was every moment of every day. He trusted in his excitingly uncertain future, and he was never embarrassed by decisions he made, even if it meant my dad finding twenty pot plants hidden in our basement. I think my father pretended to be mad, but was secretly impressed with the intelligence behind it. If you know anything about successfully growing different breeds of marijuana, it's definitely no shot in the dark (no pun intended). And don't worry, Bobby wouldn't charge you for it either. He wasn't in it for the money. I think he just loved the challenge and discipline...and maybe he even got a little high from the risk behind his illegal science experiment.

The words of Bobby's final tattoo meant living each day to the fullest and subscribing to the notion that he would relive his exact same life many times over, if given the choice. They meant "balls to the wall" and "no regrets" and "YOLO" and "#blessed" all rolled into one. That's what I think the tattoo meant for Bobby. But I had no way of knowing the significance it would come to hold for me personally in the very near future.

First, to state the obvious, it was like something out of a creepy paranormal science-fiction novel...a personalized foreshadowing from Bobby himself of his own impending death. It was as if he intentionally got that tattoo before he passed to ensure that those who loved him the most could accept this loss…this fate.

And it truly did help me accept the inconceivable turn of events. It didn't happen overnight. But eventually, after many tears, anger, soul searches and philosophical conversations, I realized that if given the choice, I would always choose to relive the 25 years I was lucky enough to spend with my brother, even if it meant I would be forced to endure the pain of losing him in every iteration. I would make that choice a million times over, if it meant I was fortunate enough to be left with the countless joyful and loving memories we made in the time we had together. Memories like spreading mashed potatoes and gravy all over our lips for a Thanksgiving Day photo, or finally sitting down at a bar next to each other after college, having whacky, deep life conversations.

Although I feel robbed by the heart-wrenching and terribly unfair loss of my brother at such a young age, I've chosen to recognize the many possible (and in my mind much worse) alternatives. I could have been an only child. We could have been separated at birth. I could have lost Bobby at the age of five to a kidnapping. Like I said, I watched too many episodes of *Unsolved Mysteries!*

But instead, I got to share 25 years with one of the most amazing humans I've ever known, and I've chosen to celebrate that. I've chosen to let go of my anger and sadness, and to be thankful for 25 years' worth of love gained through Bobby. I've chosen to love my fate.

Although miraculous in and of itself, I don't believe for a second that Bobby's tattoo was simply intended as a coping mechanism for me to survive and come to terms with his death. In true Bobby form, he used this inventive technique to teach me how to transform my outlook on my entire life – the good, the bad and the oh so ugly.

In the following years, I would face unprecedented trauma, heartache and loss. "Amor fati" would become my own personal mantra…a gift from my brother…a flashlight guiding me to find myself when I hadn't even realized I was lost. I chose to view obstacles in the context of his body art. And because I made that choice, I've become a new person that I'm certain is infinitely better than the woman I'd have been otherwise.

Bobby would be 32 years old today. He would have graduated college with a degree in horticulture. Maybe he'd be working to grow a genetically altered breed of pot to eventually cure cancer, all the while rocking out to his electronic dance music and sporting his neon green jumpsuit.

He would have attended my wedding in Jamaica in the fall of 2016, smiling his gentle smile, his eyes sparkling as he wrapped me in a hug and told me how impressed he was with my choice in destination location. But then again, who knows if I ever would have met Jack if not for Bobby's death?

For me to say that the world works in mysterious ways is an almost comical understatement, mainly because I can't rule out the possibility that Bobby's tragic fate paved the way for me to open my heart to love again. I don't like to say "everything happens for a reason" because horrible and unjust atrocities occur around the world daily, leaving me wondering if there can possibly be a God. But somehow, I still feel in the deepest depths of my soul that Bobby set the stage for my own fantastic evolution -physically, mentally and emotionally. And because of that, I can't help but love my fate…and Bobby's.

CHAPTER 1

THE DRAGONFLY

You will be met with life challenges that change your path…let them.

On October 6, 2011, everything I knew and trusted in the world was ravaged by a cruel, morbid twister. I'm not sure how such devastation can creep up so stealthily.

It was 6:00am when my cell phone started to "honky tonk" me out of a cozy, ignorant slumber. With one eyelid gradually winning the battle against the pleasant weight of sleep, I could just make out that it was "Mummy" calling. My hand barely brushed the edge of the nightstand as I tapped the "ignore" button. I'd call her back later.

But then it rang again. My stomach dropped, and all blood drained from my face in a flu-like panic. A myriad of horrible scenarios played through my mind. My mom never called me twice in a row...at least not without a silly harassing text in between. To this day, back-to-back phone calls make the hair on the back of my neck and arms prickle.

A meek greeting croaked from my throat as I gulped, trying to catch my breath. I knew I didn't want hear what she had to say because I knew it was wasn't good. There was nothing but ominous stillness on the other end of the phone for what seemed like a very long time.

"Sarah?" Oh God, now I really knew it was bad. It may sound strange, but my mom never said my name to begin a conversation unless it was some serious shit.

Her voice was whiny, but surprisingly calm. "Bobby was in a car accident, and he's very hurt." She paused to take a take a deep breath. "You need to get dressed and come with us to Connecticut as soon as you can."

I hung up the phone but remained frozen. I didn't know how to get dressed or brush my teeth. My legs didn't remember how to get me out of bed. Getting to my mom's house was like trying to navigate blindfolded in a foreign country. I commanded myself to stay calm and organize my thoughts.

Right leg in your jeans...now the left. Pick up your pocketbook. Get in the car. That's all you have to do. One step at a time.

In reality, the drive took about 20 minutes. It felt like 20 hours. My brain was a vacuum. I can't recall one coherent thought firing the entire ride, except that making a phone call to anyone terrified me. Speaking actual words was inconceivable. And even worse, spoken words would make this nightmare real.

By the time I pulled into her driveway, Mom had received some more details. Bobby was the passenger in an accident with a tractor trailer on one of the busiest highways in America. He had severe head trauma, and the medical flight had been cancelled after first responders arrived on scene. The doctor told her not to rush, but to get to hospital as soon as possible.

CANCELLED MEDFLIGHT. DON'T RUSH. In those words…in that very moment…I knew what the doctor wasn't permitted to tell us over the phone.

In the backseat behind my mom and her boyfriend, Carl, I stared out the window looking but seeing nothing in a surreal state of bewilderment. I wonder if that's how Bobby felt when he tripped on LSD? Very few words were exchanged during the almost three hours to the hospital.

"Mom, Bobby would never want to be a vegetable the rest of his life. You know that, right?" She agreed with a disoriented nod of her head. I knew she and I were grappling with the same unspoken thoughts, anticipating a a dismal prognosis and harrowing decision.

When we finally reached the hospital, we were escorted to a private waiting area "decorated" in drab white and grey tones. It spewed a clinical vibe, dull and unfriendly without an ounce of comfort. Even the couches were stiff and uninviting, like resting your bum on a wooden plank.

We waited. And then we waited some more. I kept swallowing my own spit, fighting the urge to puke. Finally, the doctor appeared, approaching us very matter-of-factly. I already knew what he was about to say.

In a soft but less than gentle whisper, he blurted, "We've never seen such bad brain trauma in all of our years in medicine. We don't even have the option of sustaining Bobby as a vegetable. There's nothing we can do. I'm so sorry."

I kept expecting to wake up. This had to be a bad dream. What does he mean? Bobby's gone? As in dead? As in never coming home again?

"Let me see him." I snapped. There was no way in hell I was leaving that hospital without seeing my brother. The doctor explained that seeing Bobby could be psychologically scarring. He questioned whether it was the best decision. I think at that moment a laugh actually escaped my lips. This guy was kidding himself if he thought for one second he'd deter me from going to Bobby.

I charged down the corridor, not even sure of the room number. There's no preparing yourself to lay eyes on your violently distorted little brother, but it was never a choice for me. "Fight or flight" had kicked in; I was running on pure adrenaline and an animalistic need to be next to my brother.

And suddenly, Bobby was laying in front of me. My heart stuttered, and my breath was trapped as if a hard candy was lodged in my chest. It wasn't Bobby. His face was eerily blank, like a corpse in an open casket. His engorged head was wrapped in gauze. At least two heads could have fit under there. I could tell he was already gone, but I immediately cradled his limp, ice-cold hand. The doctors had kept him on a ventilator until we arrived to soften the blow of seeing him as an empty, lifeless body.

The pure agony consuming me as I walked out the automatic sliding glass doors without my brother was my own personal torture chamber. I knew he was gone, but I was compelled by an indescribable force to wrap him in a blanket and hold him in my arms all the way home…or to remain by his hospital bed for all of eternity. How could we just leave him there? My little brother. My mother's son. It felt so despicably wrong to my core…like we were just letting him die. My mom, Carl, and me…driving away…leaving Bobby and his beautiful soul behind.

For the next month, I stayed with Mom and Carl. My house was a half hour away in a small, woodsy New England town – "in the sticks" as they say. I was proud to have purchased my own brand new home at the age of 23. I'd reached "independent woman" status, living there alone, single-handedly managing all bills and upkeep. None of these accomplishments seemed to matter now.

Back from the hospital with Bobby's life in the rearview mirror, I slowly maneuvered the car down my quarter mile driveway set among towering pines. I had trouble finding the strength to walk up the front stairs, much less assemble an overnight bag of matching clothes and the appropriate cosmetics. It all seemed so futile and exhausting, and the ethereal feeling of being alone with my thoughts was scary for the first time in my life. That thirty minutes seemed like an eternity, and I pathetically gasped for every breath I took, panicking my way through the blazing fire.

I just needed to get back to Mom. In retrospect, I should've had her accompany me, but I honestly couldn't have imagined that being alone would provoke such terror. I'd always been unafraid to dive headfirst into the unknown, not requiring others' approval or help along the way. I was a strong, self-sufficient woman. But this hollow, incapacitating feeling of loss was a handicap that no interview coach or personal fitness trainer could've ever lent me the coping skills to combat.

As I pulled the heavy door shut behind me, my eyes were drawn to a fluorescent green and brown dragonfly sitting on the roof of my car. Strange, I'd never noticed one hanging around in the fall before. Summertime brought swarms of them to my neck of the woods, but October wasn't exactly dragonfly season.

At that moment, I realized I'd forgotten the laundry basket of dirty clothes I planned to take care of at my mom's house that evening (funny how in the face of death and grief, my type-A brain chemistry still manages to underscore the impending need for clean clothes). Walking back down the brick path towards the house, I realized I was not alone after all. The dragonfly floated close by, gracefully accompanying me as I retraced my steps to the door. And it was there waiting for me when I returned. In fact, it followed me until my hand found the driver's side door handle.

A quick Google search will tell you that "the dragonfly, in almost every part of the world symbolizes change...in the perspective of self-realization; and the kind of change that has its source in mental and emotional maturity and the understanding of the deeper meaning of life." To me, that mid-autumn dragonfly visit was

Bobby assuring me that everything was going to be ok. It was the beginning of me realizing the gift he had left. To this day, I take comfort in the sight of a dragonfly. It reminds me that I'm strong, even when I feel I'm at my weakest. And it reminds me that the bond I share with Bobby can never die, even if he is no longer alive in the physical sense.

When I arrived back at my mom's, I could breathe again. Friends and family were constantly stopping by, filling the house with memories, laughter, family-style meals, wine, love and even more meals.

Jack, a family friend, was a constant peripheral vision. I'd never gotten to know him very well, mostly since he was off the party grid in a ten-year relationship with his high school girlfriend and wasn't around much. It was just days before Bobby's death that he'd finally asked Sabrina to move out of his house.

The night after Bobby's accident, I had an incredibly random dream about Jack. I was competing in a swim meet at the high school in the next town over (I was never a swimmer in real life), and I climbed out of the pool dripping wet. There was Jack, proudly standing with a big fluffy towel, waiting to wrap me up and dry me off. He pulled the towel around my chest and squeezed his arms tight with my head tucked perfectly into the nape of his neck.

Not only did I wake up bewildered at the thought of Jack playing the role of leading man in my dreams, but more so I was stunned by how much real-life emotion that towel hug evoked. I couldn't deny that I didn't want that moment to end.

The next night I had more dreams of Jack. We were lying on the floor close to each other, just talking. Again, this dream conjured an indescribable sense of comfort and contentment. It spurred in me an overwhelming urge to get to know Jack better. And since we were now frequently finding ourselves running in the same social circle, I could conveniently avoid being obvious with my intentions. It was all quite natural; he and I literally had something planned together every night for the next three weeks as everyone tried to keep my family busy and shower us with love and support.

One night, we all made plans to meet at a local pizza joint - a shadowy dive that, more importantly, served a wide array of beer and liquor. Jack was going to be there, and I secretly couldn't wait to run into him. After a few drinks, we found ourselves standing at a high-top table just the two of us, chatting the night away - teasing, laughing and so easily enjoying each other's company.

I had ridden to the bar with my mom, but she wanted to head home before I was ready to pull myself away. Another friend had planned to give me a lift, but Jack chirped right up to offer a ride at the end of the night, since he lived close by. We climbed into his truck, and his go-to country radio station switched on. I remember hearing Brad Paisley's "I Thought I Loved You Then" and laughing to myself thinking *What if this is the beginning of 'us?' How weird would that be? But this is Jack we're talking about. No way!*

He followed me into the house to drop some leftovers in the fridge. I could tell by the look in his eyes that he wanted to kiss me goodnight, and I know he sensed my reciprocation. But instead I blurted an awkward goodbye and darted up the stairs, leaving Jack to scurry off like a shy sixth grader.

Before my shit eating grin and I had even made it to the bedroom, my cell phone lit up. It was Jack. He didn't have my number so he'd Facebook messaged me something awfully proper and chivalrous to the effect of "I had a great time with you tonight, and I hope we can get together again soon."

I tried desperately to hold myself back just a few minutes before responding. You know, do the whole brush my teeth and not act too excited thing. But of course, I caved and wrote back almost immediately, agreeing that I'd like to spend more time together.

My next opportunity was Halloween night, and you better believe I was determined to look cute! My costume was Jillian Michaels - no shocker there, considering my passion for fitness. I made certain my yoga pants were nice and tight, since I have yet to meet a guy that doesn't appreciate a nice bum. And let me tell you, this bum in particular has been quite a work-in-progress, since I didn't get any of those glute-growing genetics. Without weight training, my butt has always looked like it got pounded by a spatula. After hours in the gym, I've finally gone from baby got no back to baby got just a lil' back. I'll take what I can get, but Kim Kardashian, you better appreciate that booty with which you were blessed!

Just as the costume party kicked off with me playfully barking orders at my family and friends to get down on the floor and give me some push-ups, the bar's kitchen caught fire. We shuffled our feet to keep warm, waiting for the fire department to give the green light to head back inside to our festivities and libations.

But something more than a kitchen fire was sparking in the chilly autumn night air. The comfortable, playful banter came so easily with Jack. And I somehow didn't mind one bit that I was looking at a very different version than the handsome, charming, clean-cut young man that had driven me home the week before.

Let's just say he wasn't the best-looking guy at the bar that night with his redneck flannel lumberjack costume - complete with fake crooked teeth, some goofy hillbilly hat, tin foil axe, and a pair of extra-long denim shorts that I believe the wise-ass yuppies refer to as "jorts" nowadays.

Actually, I take that back. The outfit I could deal with, but the dental work was just horrendous. In addition to the extreme organization and cleanliness that comes with my personality, I've always been one to notice an especially good (or bad) set of teeth, particularly when it comes to a romantic interest. And Halloween Jack looked like someone had punched out a stranger's set of decaying teeth, collected a haphazard handful, and tossed them sloppily into his mouth. That grotesque set of fake chompers was truly something out of my dating nightmares!

We became impatient and decided to head to a nearby pub whose kitchen wasn't currently engulfed in flames. I was feeling especially fun and frisky at our next stop, and decided to challenge Jack to drink some shots.

In hindsight, this wasn't the best idea since the shock and anguish of Bobby's passing had left me with very little appetite, and taking care of myself wasn't exactly a top priority in those weeks. It was as if the loss and grief took up all of the available space in my brain and stomach. But inevitably Jack's warm, friendly and funny demeanor had somehow made room for the proverbial flirtatious butterflies of a new crush.

As we clinked and threw back one pair of shot glasses after another, I caught a good buzz. And then suddenly I was rip roaring drunk. The bar had become an inebriated blur of sexy black cats, spooky horror masks, jack-o-lantern shadows, booming country music, clumsy dance moves and boisterous laughter.

I was later told that Jack and I were aggressively making out in the back seat of his friend's car on the drive home.

Yikes! I can't imagine I was the classiest or most skillful of kissers that night. I couldn't even formulate a sentence, much less control my drool that I'm sure was dripping down the collar of Jack's plaid flannel shirt. But it seems that the rare occurrence of me not speaking worked in my favor, since it somehow got my ass back to his house. And boom. Lights out. That's all she wrote. Or not...

I woke up late the next morning in boxer shorts and an oversized men's t-shirt, hearing the gentle sloshing of a washing machine in a distant corner of the house. I somehow knew my clothes were in that washing machine...and I knew it wasn't a good sign.

As I tried to focus my vision and lift my pounding head from the pillow, Jack emerged from the kitchen holding two mugs of fresh pumpkin spice coffee, and proceeded to explain (in entirely too cheerful a manner) that once we arrived back at his place, our make out session had quickly transformed into my own personal Halloween horror show. My tight-ass-pants-wearing, frisky, fun self had vomited profusely all over both of us, as well as his brand new bedroom comforter.

Jack chuckled proudly as he described his accomplishment of guiding a disoriented and unsteady Jillian Michaels to the shower to help clean her up. And that's when things got *really* interesting!

To my horror, I learned that once in the shower, I'd completely lost all bodily control (yes, that means exactly what you're thinking it does)! And just a few hours earlier, I'd been hung up on some bad fake teeth?! Oops.

But Jack didn't seem fazed one bit by my bodily misfires, and after I'd choked down a couple sips of water and some ibuprofen, he left me to sleep it off in his bed. Not only that, but he continued to check in and snuggle throughout the rest of the day. Maybe I was too hungover to care what a train wreck I'd been the night before. Or maybe it was something about Jack's caring and accepting nature that couldn't help but make me feel comfortable and content. All I knew was that I was sweating stale booze out of my pores and probably reeked like a Sunday morning frat house, but I somehow couldn't muster up any feelings of real embarrassment.

Around mid-afternoon, I began to feel somewhat human and gradually made my way back to an upright position. I found the energy to put on my freshly laundered walk-of-shame attire, and began the sluggish trek home to my own couch. As I stood in Jack's doorway thanking him one last time for his superhuman patience and unprecedented hospitality, he surprised me by asking if I wanted to come back to hang out later that night. I gladly took him up on his invitation, and he continued to invite me over almost every night after.

Over the next six years, Jack and I developed a relationship different than any I'd experienced. We became companions of leisure, exploring numerous exotic locations around the world. Our spontaneous adventures included concerts, beach getaways, ski resorts, paddle boards, new cuisines and endless cocktails. Reveling in the young "double income no kids" freedom that we shared and our immediate level of comfort with one another gave me a sense of happiness and fulfillment when I needed it most.

We eventually moved in together, and I even became a dog owner, adopting his six-year-old chocolate lab as my own. This concept may not seem all that significant to some. But for this neat freak, coexisting with a large, dark-haired canine has been a true personal accomplishment. For someone who has dealt with so many life challenges, I'm still not sure why pet dander seems mentally harder than the rest.

In the winter of 2016, Jack proposed at our favorite Caribbean resort, and we returned to that same location the following year for a spectacular Jamaican wedding celebration. Our barefoot beach ceremony and week-long vacation was paradise on earth, and I could not be more thankful to have been surrounded by so many friends and family offering their profound love and support.

Although our relationship was not perfect and has changed in almost indescribable ways, I think Jack was absolutely part of my plan. He was the blessing waiting for me at the end of all the pain. I had never met someone like him, and our first "romantic" encounter was definitely not the way I had envisioned it all falling into place.

Remember that aside from the fact that my first night with him was spent like a 21st birthday after-party, he was almost like family to me before we were romantically involved.

We faced our fair share of criticism from others when we began dating, and some even tried to break us up. In previous years I probably would have cared a lot about what these haters thought of my life. I may have even allowed the opinions of others to ruin my relationship. This time, I didn't care.

Losing Bobby had somehow made me lose all fear of what could happen if I did or didn't do what others expected of me or deemed acceptable. It taught me to live for my own happiness and no one else's because life is short, and you never know how many days you have left to soak it up. It gave me an odd sense of freedom and confidence, and I took a chance on a once in a lifetime experience with a man I loved because of it.

I truly wish I could pass this mindset onto everyone in the world, while withholding the pain it took me to get here. I can't for the life of me understand why anyone wants to steal true happiness from their fellow human being. If you're currently tolerating people in your life who have anything other than unwavering support for you (whether you're at your worst or best), then I strongly advise reconsidering these relationships.

Those who are truly fulfilled and confident in their life choices aim to surround themselves with others who project the same.

As far as I'm concerned, those closest to you should always be your biggest fans. If they aren't, it most likely stems from jealously or their own lack of fulfillment, and you should be sure to tell them they need to go pick another team.

This notion rings equally true in both personal and professional relationships. I've learned that associating with those who aim to bring you down just to lift themselves up will inevitably decrease your self-confidence and chances of sharing your gifts with the world. Don't let their negativity scare you away from being your genuine self. Don't let them hinder the spirit burning inside you.

In short, don't let the ugly fake redneck teeth get in your head or blind you from the bigger picture and your chance at a happy life. Follow your inner dragonfly wherever it leads you. You know it better than you think. It's that feeling in your gut...in your heart...telling you that you're exactly where you're supposed to be in this moment. I know Bobby has been watching my next chapters unfold, and maybe even orchestrating them in some way.

CHAPTER 2

A MOTHER'S TOUCH

For every joy, there exists equal and opposite pain. BUT joy always trumps pain, and they work together to make you grow.

The Cape Cod Canal has always been a personal haven for me to escape with my thoughts and have easy conversations with those I love. The navy blue sparkling water and smooth paved bike path stretch for seven miles from Buzzards Bay to Sandwich, frequented by walkers, runners, cyclists, fishermen and other energetic nature lovers. Of course, you occasionally come across the more lethargic looking canal goers, usually younger in age, whose pink glassy eyes and skunky aroma suggest that they're more enthusiastic about those gifts from Mother Nature that can be smoked. As a health and fitness buff, the canal has always been a place of positive energy, motion and rejuvenation for me. But hey, I don't judge. Everyone and everything I see, smell, taste and feel when I'm there is all part of the experience, and while not quite as entertaining as the airport, the Canal path can make for some great people watching on a nice day.

My mom and I were enjoying a cool ocean breeze cutting through the sizzling summer heat as we power walked side-by-side along the water, engrossed in delightfully mindless chatter. But, as it always did, our exchange of local restaurant recommendations and favorite seasonal cocktails inevitably changed to the deeper topics of life, or rather the tribulations of my mother's life.

Mom is so easily loveable. But she maintains a heightened particularity in who she chooses to allow into her world, which may appear alienating to those who aren't lucky enough to know her well. She's quite shy in groups, and she carries scars of distrust I can see reflected in her eyes. It's no surprise that she eludes this aloof aura after growing up in a home with an alcoholic mother and having the figurative rug ripped right out from underneath her in not one, but two distrustful marriages.

But with me, she loses that distant persona and quiet nature. With me she opens up as an honest confident and playful best friend. My perception of her is simply that of the perfect mom who packed my lunch with love every single day until I left for college.

She devoted her life to ensuring that Bobby and I were happy in every way. I couldn't wait for my dad to go hunting each year after Thanksgiving because that meant we got to sleep upstairs in the king size bed alongside Mom. It meant we didn't have a bedtime. It meant that in the morning, she would make us our favorite breakfast, in the afternoon our favorite lunch, and in the evening our favorite dinner. I can still smell the freshly toasted pumpernickel bagels loaded with tuna salad (made only with Hellmann's mayonnaise, of course). But I promise my mom did so much more than just feed us!

She and I shared a ritual of sitting on the cushy carpeted floor of my excessively pink bedroom, combing through my clothes to see which I'd grown out of. She'd make piles of what was to be donated and what I could still wear, and then write an organized list of what she needed to buy for me. I can honestly say I don't remember a time when I didn't have something I needed. Her innate ability to plan ahead for our family made it appear that she had lived this life a million times before. She was an expert at keeping everyone and everything organized. If my dad needed a receipt from ten years before, she could pull it out within 60 seconds. She always made it look so easy too, like a magical little curly black-haired fairy.

I would beg her every night to tickle my back before I fell asleep, and she rarely objected. I'd cocoon myself in my pastel heart patterned comforter and lay in my canopy bed eagerly awaiting my nighttime indulgence. We'd chat about school and other happenings, or the following day's plans, until I was so relaxed that I could no longer hold a conversation. It was the perfect way to decompress and fall asleep – soaking up the comfort of a mother's touch. There's nothing like it.

Now, as her arms pumped back and forth and beads of sweat collected on her forehead, I listened to her reminisce that having children with my father was one of the greatest joys of her life. She went on to describe how her second marriage also brought her ten years of love and happiness that she'd never before experienced with a man.

No longer a little girl with pink walls and pastel hearts shielding me from the reality of the adult world, I'm privy to Mom's emotional and physical suffering. Both of her husbands' bad decisions somehow seemed to take precedence over her health and happiness. It compels me to ask her, "Would you do it all over again?"

She responds immediately with a resounding "Absolutely."

She amazes me.

Her first marriage of over twenty years to my father crumbled after decades of trying to rebuild broken trust over and over. A few years later, her son passed away at the young age of 25, and she was diagnosed with breast cancer just a year later (which I'm sure was in part a result of stress). Post-cancer, her second marriage also ended with a defeat of trust. It leaves me in awe that even after all of this misery, the resilience of the human spirit has made it possible for my mother to remember more of the good than the bad. And furthermore, she wouldn't change a thing if given the choice!

As she sees it, she wouldn't have had my brother and me without her marriage to my dad. And perhaps her second husband coming into her life was intended as a method of survival and moving forward from the collapse of the life she knew for 20+ years. She miraculously keeps the memories of love and joy that Carl brought at the forefront of her mind, instead of resentfully focusing on the way he hurt her. And the end of that relationship will inevitably lead her to the next phase of her life's happiness, whatever that may be. There will undoubtedly be more sadness and suffering in her future, but that pain will also bring with it equal and opposite joy, as she has seen time and time again.

Although very hard to witness, my mother's intense personal challenges have helped teach me that the greatest joys can be defined by the worst pain. You're on cloud nine at certain moments throughout life, with the ever-present risk that the cloud can vanish in an instant. But the important thing to recognize is that you almost always come away with something valuable from a loss (whether a child, romantic relationship, memory or lesson learned). One would not exist without the other.

I too have found in my personal experience that without some of the most intense suffering, the most profound joy would cease to exist; it is somehow possible for a higher happiness to exist after such crippling pain. And I'm not talking about the pain of doing pushups or nursing a hangover. I'm talking about the kind of pain that takes away a piece of your soul. The kind that leaves you gasping for breath, struggling to salvage the tiniest trace of resilience left inside you. This sort of agony, although debilitating in the moment (and in many cases for several years at a time), can bring with it some surprisingly positive life transformations - largely because real trauma has a funny way of freeing you from the more insignificant worries in the long-run.

Watching my parents' marriage implode, experiencing the death of my little brother, and standing by Mom's side as she suffered through months of chemotherapy jarred my mind, body and soul into an indescribable state of vulnerability, clarity and eventually courage. It seems a cruel irony that my worst nightmares and greatest life tragedies pushed my brain into a permanent state of infinite possibility with virtually no fear. But that is precisely what happened, and I will forever be grateful.

My entire attitude changed for the better, fueled by positivity and a new-found outlook that anything is possible. I no longer let sitting in traffic ruin my day. Someone's brother may have died in that car accident that has EMTs blocking the right-hand lane. And I feel virtually no intimidation at the thought of an upcoming job interview because nothing any hiring manager throws at me can be nearly as challenging as trying to find the words to say to my own father as he's standing in front of me admitting to sleeping with other women shortly before coming home to Mom's home-cooked meal.

Making a conscious decision to embrace this personal growth and look at life with a "glass half full" mentality has allowed me to find a sense of contentment that I never knew possible.

Now please don't mistake my sentiments as me wishing hurt or loss on anyone. I am however, accepting the reality that hurt and loss are mandatory parts of life, and they can work to improve your character in a way you would never anticipate.

What about you? Would you relive the greatest joys in your life if you knew it also meant enduring the greatest hurt? Most of us (or at least those who don't live merely to drive fancy cars and carry Louis Vuitton bags) equate the greatest happiness to the relationships we build - meeting your soulmate, getting engaged, marriage, having a family, getting a puppy, watching your grandchildren grow. Would you have gotten married if you knew you were going to lose your husband to another woman? Would you have had a baby if you knew he was going to die in a car accident at the age of 25? Would you have spent a long weekend away with your lover if you knew you could never truly be together in the end? Would you still buy the puppy even though you'd eventually have to be driven to the vet to have it put down? Just like my mom, the answer is likely an immediate and resounding "Absolutely" because some of the darkest days are also a pathway to some of the most beautiful.

Choosing to appreciate life's gifts in the face of pain and suffering will condition you to be infinitely grateful and fearless. But more importantly, you'll nurture your ability to focus on the light at the end of the tunnel during the most hopeless of times.

CHAPTER 3

SHINING YOUR LIGHTBULB

Don't let another person's fear rub off on you.

Have you ever been in a group setting where you suddenly find yourself eagerly sharing very personal ideas, goals and dreams? Well apparently I was born with some kind of genetic predisposition to do so because I find myself in this kind of situation quite frequently.

As I've mentioned, I love to talk; exchanging energy and ideas with others gives me some kind of natural high. I don't know how else to describe it. My conversations always seem to get to a much deeper level than the average person. Let's just say if you're meeting me out for a drink, you should never expect to discuss topics like how unseasonably warm it's been for fall in New England, or how exciting it is that Vera Bradley is having a trunk show in town next week. More likely topics of our girlfriends' night out will be theories on why the divorce rate is so high, or the profound effects (both physical and mental) that probiotics have been found to have on human health.

If you can relate and you've experienced genuine excitement to share a thought or idea with others, were you ever met with an extremely negative initial reaction, such as the rolling of eyes, or maybe even a snarky laugh?

Let me first say that I wholeheartedly recognize the colossal value of human reflection, discussion, debate, the offering of real opinions, and constructive criticism...BUT only when it comes from a benevolent place. One of my biggest pet peeves is when someone puts themselves out there to share an idea, and other people laugh or quickly (and rudely) discount it.

This kind of judgmental person simply doesn't last long in my life. Why? Because their ridicule is a direct reflection of their lack of confidence in their own ideas and what they have to offer the world. Most likely, they lack the courage to risk the kind of vulnerability that comes with tossing a "crazy" idea out there, much less to act on it. The real reason behind that quick, cynical discrediting of someone else's vision is probably that they themselves are too scared of everything they can't find the courage to share and do in life. They are terrified of rejection and failure, so they project their fear onto you, in hopes that you won't prove to be a braver, more successful person than they are. Misery and complacency love company.

I've found there are a few things that successful and fulfilled people have in common. They maintain a positive self-image, practice positive self-suggestion, aren't afraid to take a chance (and fail), and they encourage others to follow suit. I'm pretty sure lots of people laughed when Thomas Edison first tossed out his idea of the light bulb, but that clearly didn't stop him...thank God!

To clarify, I'm not suggesting being careless or making ridiculously stupid choices, like deciding it's a brilliant idea to follow the "eat nothing but celery" two-week cleanse. I'm suggesting you listen to those little voices in your head pushing you to network with marketing companies seeking freelance writers like you've been saying you want to do for the past ten years. Listen to those creative voices, those burning desires urging you to quit the corporate job you loathe, even though it offers a reliable salary with great benefits. Following your passion for baking and opening your own cake shop may seem like a crazy impulsive move, but imagine your new life if you succeed.

What is the worst that can happen? If you go into anything with the best of intentions and give 100% to make your dream a reality, some good will undoubtedly come out of it. It may not be the good you'd predicted, but the good WILL come.

One of my favorite Country music songs is "Road Less Traveled" by Lauren Alaina. It articulates my message perfectly. One particularly insightful verse advises:

"You won't make yourself a name if you follow the rules.
History gets made when you're acting a fool.
So, don't hold it back and just run it...
Show what you got and just own it."

Lauren, my friend, you nailed it. The naysayers are harboring too much fear of their own seemingly whacky ideas to own them, take the chance and "run it."

The sooner people realize this, the sooner they will stop seeking the validation of others, and put their own goals into motion...no matter how unfathomable they may seem in the here and now. Someday, you may very well find yourself looking back and laughing at this current version of you...laughing at how unsure you were that your idea could ever become a reality. And now look at you, eager to get out of bed every morning and write that article or bake that wedding cake, living comfortably doing what you love. You did it because you put your fear (and the fear projected through the scornful laughter of others) aside to take a chance on what you believed was possible.

Well, I've got news for you...this concept doesn't stop in the realm of scientific invention or career moves. Remaining honest and open with others about your personal dreams, wins, losses and state of mind (including the most brutal emotional battles you've faced) will bring you the highest degree of living.

Shortly after Bobby died and I started staying with Jack, I joined the local gym. I wanted to get my endorphins firing again, and ensure that I was proactively supporting my body, mind and overall personal health through diet and exercise. I knew it would help me mentally as I worked to overcome this life-altering tragedy.

My gym membership introduced me to a new network of people, useful for more so much more than communicating fitness and diet tips. The gym opened up a brand new social circle of interesting (and some not so interesting) minds that for the most part, I couldn't help but be excited to explore.

I chose not to take any prescription drugs like anti-depressants, and I made the conscious decision not to shut anyone out, no matter how shitty I felt. I openly shared my thoughts and feelings with friends, family, fellow gym-goers, co-workers, and even strangers, though I knew I was risking their perceptions of me as unnerving or weird for being so raw. I even cried in front of people I didn't know. And then the strangest thing happened. People started telling me their stories back.

It astonished me how many people in my life had been through similar events without sharing them with anyone...ever?! Some had lost siblings as children, or even their own child during birth. I guess they just didn't think anyone could possibly understand their loss, or want to hear their "sob story," at the risk of being pegged as whiny…weak…different.

But it was refreshingly the exact opposite! The more honest conversations I had with others about my life challenges, the more people opened up to me with their own incredible stories. We established a relationship - a bond as they were pleasantly surprised that their experiences didn't make them different than others at all….these experiences made them inherently the same.

Human beings yearn to connect with other human beings....REAL people who share themselves - the good, the bad and the ugly, no matter how vulnerable it may prove them to be. We are all innately human - sometimes weak, sometimes strong...but always carrying faults and failures to which others (even complete strangers) can relate. This is the beauty in the bond of humanity.

Now, I am not naïve, and I definitely don't expect that every personality on the planet will ever be as comfortable as I am in sharing personal heartaches and skeletons. But after my experience fearlessly sharing the life events that have most deeply affected me (for better or for worse), I know without a doubt that there are always more people than you'd expect experiencing something similar to what you're going through. ALWAYS. You are NEVER alone.

Don't let fear convince you otherwise. Don't allow it to stunt your expression of those brilliant unrealized, ready-to-be-born ideas, inventions, motivations, feelings, stories, jokes, goofy laughter, or uncontrollable tears. These are the very elements that contribute to the truest form of human connection, and that connection – that support from complex, thinking, feeling, breathing human beings just like you is what makes life worth living.

Be brave enough to dispel the fear that others often attempt to project onto you, and proudly share whatever it is that you have to offer. More often than not, you'll be met with the support of another human spirit who can relate to you. Support always creates strength, and I have yet to find one aspect of life in which this is untrue.

CHAPTER 4

GIRL CRUSHING IT

Support creates strength...and a damn good business model.

As I dove headfirst into the fulfilling fitness grind and focusing more on nutrition, I joined a boot camp workout class that met twice a week for intense interval training.

Sonya was a regular class participant, and became a familiar face (and perfectly sun-kissed toned body). She'd been a few years behind Jack in high school, and was the epitome of a "girl boss" - a fitness badass who had recently placed in a few local and national figure competitions. Let me tell you that if this girl lifted her shirt, you could truly scrub out your laundry on her beautifully defined abs. And not only that, she also happens to be intelligent, driven and absolutely stunning. A great combination of strong and sexy (I promise I'm heterosexual).

I'd lost weight, muscle, and strength in the months after my brother's passing. Most women would probably rejoice at the idea of the bathroom scale reflecting a lower number, but this is a perfect example of how weight loss isn't always a good thing. My skin was loose, and I felt pathetically weak. I longed to have my old firm body and strength back, and I knew that teaming up with up someone else always makes things more fun for me.

Sonya was the perfect motivational workout buddy when her busy schedule as a single mom and sales professional allowed it. But in between the school fundraisers and work travel, she always somehow seemed to make it work beautifully. And she always made the time for consistent workouts. She had a real passion for the gym, staying fit and sharing her killer weight-training routines, lucky for me!

During our exercise sessions, Sonya made sure to point out exactly which muscle we were building in that day's routine. It kept me fired up and gave me infinite inspiration, as I found myself always looking forward to the next workout and muscle group on the schedule. In between sets, we gabbed about typical girl stuff – skin care regimens, romantic relationships, great shopping deals…you name it. We quickly became the best of gym buddies and genuine friends.

Sonya and I were meeting at the gym almost daily, eager to launch into a new workout, as well as our in-between-sets chat sessions. The workouts flew by. I enjoyed them so much that they never actually felt like working out at all, except ironically, I was pushing my body further than I had in my life. Sonya and I complimented each other, respected each other and most of all accepted each other. We had different bodies, different personalities and different goals. And guess how much all of those differences mattered? Not one bit. Sonya was my biggest fan – always encouraging me to work towards whatever goals my kooky impulsive brain came up with on any given day.

At one point I was actually texting her my daily food diary to ensure I held myself accountable with clean eating habits. I'd be parked in front of a dental office (I was in dental sales at the time) sending her photos of my healthy food prep Tupperware meals. I'm sure everyone waits with bated breath for their friend's daily reports featuring turkey burger, green beans and sweet potato, right? This is invigorating stuff people! Nonetheless, Sonya never failed to respond with an enthusiastic and supportive comment.

For the first time ever, fitness and nutrition became fun. I felt healthy, strong and confident. I loved the sense of community, accountability and support that Sonya and I had built.

And so, my wheels started turning. How could we reproduce this feeling on a global scale so others could feel the same invigoration to change their lives that I had?

As a millennial raised in a world fueled by genius technological progress and social media obsession, an app was the obvious answer. My concept would allow users to group together with friends, family, co-workers and gym buddies to work towards a common goal - a healthier body, mind and soul.

After calmly listening to me pitch my idea at warp speed, Sonya (the more rational, detail-oriented of our duo) suggested that our first step be to test the model concept in a Facebook group.

Genius!

And that's exactly what we did. We invited fifteen women into a private trial group, cleverly named "YourGymGF."

Scattered all across the U.S., with some not even knowing each other, members were given an established timeline to post goals of their choice - weight loss, muscle gain, clean eating, meal prep, combating anxiety and depression (any personal target) - and then asked to post weekly progress updates.

The results were amazing. Not only did these women post their goals and updates, they quickly started posting multiple times a day, sharing workouts, recipes, motivation, successes and failures. We truly became a team growing together…and that's when the brand YourGymGF was born.

The successful results Sonya and I had seen between the two of us had multiplied with an increased number of participants. We knew it worked, and we were convinced we could make the app a reality.

CHAPTER 5

PRIME INVESTMENTS

Choose to see your lack of knowledge as an opportunity for learning and growth.

The YourGymGF app? What?! Was this real life? Do you think Sonya and I had one bit of software experience? Nope, we sure didn't. Thankfully, I love to ask questions, and we quickly learned that most people love to share knowledge.

We reached out to a few friends (and friends of friends) to gain a basic understanding of the app development process. And before we knew it, we had mock-up screen shots and a developer on board in San Francisco to help us launch the project.

We knew from the start that this business venture was not going to be easy…or cheap. It cost both Sonya and me thousands of dollars just to put this idea into motion. Not to mention, I made the decision to leave my dental sales position so I could dedicate more time to jump start the s-corporation and aggressively market our brand.

I'd suddenly gone from full-time sales account rep networking with several prominent dentists' office every day, to part-time server at a popular local restaurant. I spent a year running lobster, fish, steaks and countless cocktails to floods of tourists and locals who frequented my hometown's bustling waterfront center.

When I wasn't at the restaurant, I dedicated every ounce of my attention to the app. We lived it, we breathed it. And guess what? The end product sucked. We were horrified to learn that our initial developer had promised us a product he couldn't deliver…and after almost three years of grueling product development, intense anticipation, impatience, overwhelming peer support, and personal investments of time, energy and money, we couldn't have been more disappointed. What a waste.

But after our initial bout of anger and self-pity had run its course, our true characters built on intelligence, determination and endless positivity emerged. We realized that through the launch of our first "blah" app, we'd built a social media following of over 20,000 people.

We were sharing healthy recipes, fitness tips, motivation and inspiring stories daily…and people were embracing it wholeheartedly! Locals began to recognize the brand, and we even sold apparel at gyms in the area. But perhaps the most rewarding returns we've seen since the inception of YourGymGF were the countless messages and overwhelmingly positive feedback on the impact of our frankly, still intangible product.

A true entrepreneur would likely ask "Well so what? What is that worth?" Although there isn't much monetary value outside of the workout apparel sold (which is nowhere near making us a profit), I'm not bullshitting you when I say that for us, making the lives of others happier and healthier doesn't carry a price tag.

But let's keep it real here...we didn't sacrifice our jobs, personal time and savings to be paid in smiles, hugs and warm fuzzy feelings from our local gym buddies and high school friends. We knew the momentum of the community brand we'd built wasn't really going to take off to meet its true potential unless we took a new direction. So, we decided to seek out a new developer.

At this stage, I was so eager for more information that I actually had the balls to solicit a prestigious software company in Boston, creepily making my way up the elevator past the diligently working employees and directly to the desk of the CEO. He had NO idea how I got there, but he was so impressed with my determination that he actually gave me a few minutes of his time. He was wearing jeans - the most laid-back businessman I'd ever seen. He asked a few questions about the app, and we discussed overall goals. I remember the pride I felt that my cloak-and-dagger excursion had earned me a few tips from his entrepreneurial genius.

I also vividly remember my biggest takeaway from that brief conversation - the horrific realization that it would easily cost Sonya and me another $200k+ to bring our company to life. We didn't have that sort of cash flow, but we still weren't willing to throw in the towel.

We needed a new developer, and my next move was a simple appeal to the Facebook community - "Does anyone have connections at MIT?"

Within a few hours, I'd received a private message from a high school friend, an MIT employee. He had a few software engineer connections, including a New Hampshire developer looking to take on new projects for equity. I'm pretty sure that developer thought I was a complete wacko during our initial phone conversation, but he could also no doubt sense the determination and passion in my voice.

He agreed to meet with us, and Sonya and I agreed that we weren't letting him leave that restaurant without signing onto this project. I like to think our refined sales skills were the reason we closed that deal. However, our palpable passion and thirst for knowledge was more likely what compelled him to work with us. And so the app development process began again from square one!

CHAPTER 6

A CHAMPION TRACK RECORD

Don't be afraid to take a risk if you've done your homework, proven your credibility and commit to maintaining your integrity.

Let me tell you I certainly didn't receive many positive reactions after leaving a dental sales position to dedicate my time and energy to YourGymGF. And at first glance, I can understand why. I had an amazing job with a great salary, company car, flexible schedule and full benefits. Why in God's name would I want to waitress for a year without the security of a regular paycheck, health insurance, etc. etc.?

The best way I can find to explain what motivated my seemingly irrational life decision is to say that creating a product or brand is kind of like having a baby. Now, before all you parents go ape shit on me, I admit my analogy is not exactly spot on. I don't have any children of my own just yet, but I know enough to know that very few things in the world are as intense as the love and commitment a parent has for their kid.

Let me ask you this…you 'd do anything for your children if it brought them happiness and success, right? Well, in the months that the YourGymGF business was first coming to life, I could feel myself giving birth to a very similar level of passion and commitment that I'd never before experienced.

My mind raced all day and night with endless new "crazy" ideas, from app functionality to promotional techniques. It was like I'd developed a wonderful and exciting case of Obsessive-Compulsive Disorder, and every cell in my body was working overtime, pushing me forward to make this concept a reality. I became so invested in the success of this dream, that I knew without a doubt I was making the right decision moving "backwards" to become "just a waitress." In a short time, this business had become my offspring, and there wasn't much I wouldn't do to see it thrive.

Keep in mind that I'd never in my 31 years of life considered embarking on an entrepreneurial endeavor like this, especially to launch a product so far outside the realm of my inherent knowledge and experience. But nonetheless, once the wheels were in motion, I felt like I had always been meant to go this route of creating something from nothing - something I could witness truly helping others, and of which I could be sincerely proud (and maybe even make a buck).

Who would've thought I'd find myself here? Certainly not I. But I was high on my newfound energy and the endless possibilities that lay ahead....and I loved every minute of it.

Again, amor fati Bobby! Thank you, dear brother.

I was ready to hit the ground running to say the least. Unfortunately, due to previously mentioned false promises from the first developer, and the second quitting on us just before the app was complete, I never had the chance to do so.

I can't even count the hours Sonya and I spent on the phone with those guys – often from the other side of the country, at all hours of the night with someone who could barely speak English. The word "frustrating" doesn't do justice. In fact, there may not be words to describe the feeling of watching a dream like that slip away, when all of your blood sweat and tears appear to have been wasted.

Although our true vision of the app will never exist, I managed to build so much through that "failure." I spent countless hours working to create the foundation for our brand, and essentially gave myself a Master's degree in creating an s-corporation. I could never have imagined that launching a company would take so much time and energy. From opening bank accounts, accounting responsibilities, tax filings, acquiring a trademark and patent, filing never-ending legal documents and more, it was by far my most challenging homework assignment. I spent less energy getting my undergraduate degree in marketing, and no lie, I was busier than I'd ever been at a full-time job.

I also met some pretty amazing people working at the restaurant who, to this day, support my journey helping others better themselves through health and wellness, no matter the brand.

After a year of setting up the business and still waiting for the app to officially launch, I knew it was time to get back into sales. I called the recruiter I'd kept in touch with since my first position out of college and gave her the go-ahead to start hunting. I secured a pharmaceutical nutritional therapy sales position within two weeks of that phone call. Not only did the new job have better pay than my previous position, but I absolutely loved my new manager, and was much happier with the overall daily routine of this job in comparison to my last.

Some people may say I got lucky, but that's simply not the case. I had a track record of hard work and documented success, I stayed in touch with my recruiter every year to update her on where I was and how I was performing, and I left my old position on the most honest and sincere of terms. I didn't burn one single bridge, and I was determined to remain transparent with every person who helped me along the way.

I can't stress enough that there is never any harm in trying something new or leaving something comfortable behind, as long as you have a few simple (but crucial) boxes checked off.

First, make sure you've done your due diligence researching, absorbing and understanding as much as you possibly can about what that next chapter will entail and require of you. Of course, you can never be truly prepared for what lies ahead when you embark on a new challenge. And who would really want to? That's part of the fun! But gaining as much knowledge before taking the leap will surely help you along the way. Read the online articles and "how-to" guides, use your networking contacts, ask endless questions, sneak into a CEO's office…be a sponge!

It's equally important when making a big move (whether career or otherwise) to do so knowing that you've proven your skill and success in your previous endeavors. Not only will this lend you credibility amongst your peers, but the sense of personal confidence you've gained will inevitably shine through and propel you into your next adventure.

However, remember that skills and success can mean many different things for different people. They cannot be measured using one uniform method across the board. The unique nuances of human personalities, strengths and weaknesses are far too subjective for that.

For instance, many people you know have likely made money their defining factor of success, while others may choose to quantify their accomplishments (and fulfillment) in the number of new and exciting locations they've traveled to this year. Then there are those who measure life achievement using less tangible factors, such as their ability to communicate with others, skills interacting as part of a team or merely their ability to maintain balance in their life while paying the bills, staying physically fit and spending quality time with their loved ones. My point? There is no absolute success scale!

My (career) skill set was selling, which really just boils down to:

1. Being a natural extrovert, or "people person."

2. Remaining flexible and able to adapt quickly to whatever the day might throw at me without getting thrown off my game.

3. Practicing consistent self-motivation. For instance, getting up on time and out on the road when no one is standing over me forcing me to do it. Or, continuing to drop in on that one

elusive prospect who never takes the time to see me because any day may be the one he decides to hear me out and become one of my biggest sales yet.

4. Embracing my infinite sense of excitement and hunger for the next challenge ahead. Some may see this as merely being born with a competitive nature, but it's really a step further than that...it's my conscious choice to escape complacency, live my life to its fullest, and be the best possible version of myself. In a sense, yes it involves being competitive. But I'm

really only competing with myself to ensure I'm always ending the day better than I was the day before.

These personal strengths brought me success in my sales career, building me a positive reputation amongst my colleagues and friends. And once I was ready to take the leap into the YourGymGF venture, these people knew me, my skills, successes and work ethic well enough to know that I was worth the investment, whether of their money, time or simply emotional support. Although I was inevitably met with some skepticism and doubt, I had a solid squad (of both professional and personal contacts) who knew my track record.

They knew I was not going to fail in any way over which I had control, whether I was launching a fitness app or opening a lemonade stand in my driveway.

Although research and credibility should be two of the key factors driving you as you embark on any new journey, my final (and perhaps most important) ingredient in the recipe for a successful transition is integrity. Always remain true to who you are at your core, keep your word, and remain honest about EVERYTHING to those who matter – this means full transparency in your intentions, confidence, doubts, successes and failures...all of it. I can think of very few situations where being honest will hurt your success in the long run.

If I hadn't kept in touch with my recruiter all these years, or if I had left my dental sales position without an honest explanation of my future goals and on bad terms with my manager, I would've found myself having a much harder time finding new sales career opportunities and lacking strong character references when I made my way back to the industry.

So, although trying something new will most likely seem a little risky, frightening or just downright crazy, trust yourself in making these big life decisions. No one except you will be the one living with the resulting failure or success.

There's always another world of opportunity on the other side of the proverbial fence, and sometimes peaking over is scary. But if you never peak, you can guarantee you'll never find more. And if you're brave enough to take that leap and explore an unknown landscape, be sure you have my three guiding principles tucked in your back pocket.

Very rarely will things turn out as your planned, and you might even fail miserably. But this road map will undoubtedly increase your chances of success. If you never try, you'll always wonder what could have been. And that

to me is the scariest way of all to live life.

CHAPTER 7

SWALLOWING THE FROG

You can't begin the next chapter of your life if you keep re-reading the previous pages.

Are you fulfilled in your current relationship? Are you happy at your job? Are you spending sufficient quality time with loving, loyal and supportive? Are you generally healthy and thriving in mind, body and spirit? Do you feel content, optimistic and #blessed when you lay your head down on the pillow at the end of most days?

If you answered yes to all of these questions, then that's just fabulous! You're slaying this thing called life, and you, my friend, are leaps and bounds ahead of the majority of Earth's population.

Checking off all of these boxes may seem unattainable in today's fast-paced world fueled by social media, fake news, self-medication and a rapidly increasing cost of living. However, if you answered no to any of these questions, then you seriously need to ask yourself why??

What exactly is it that's causing you to be anything less than thrilled to get out of bed every morning? Because let's be honest, for the most part, we do get to choose the lives that we lead. And there is simply no justifiable reason to continue living a lower quality of life than you know you deserve.

Now let's be clear...shit happens. Layoffs occur, disease strikes, tragic accidents blindside us and natural disasters wreak havoc on nations around the globe. Literally everyone in the world has some level of unavoidable problems. Even if you're the richest man in the world, the hottest actress or the latest recipient of the Nobel Peace Prize, you still undoubtedly have genuine challenges to face on a daily basis. But that doesn't necessarily mean you're living unhappily.

The beauty of life is that no matter what uncontrollable circumstances may come our way, we still have every ounce of control over how we choose react to them. And recognizing this early on is the true key to personal growth and happiness for the majority of your existence. I know, I know…I sound like a bunch of inspirational memes on repeat, but the corniness doesn't change the fact that this is all undeniably true.

NOTHING is going to change if you keep making the same choices and doing the same things over and over again. We've all heard it – this is literally the definition of insanity (and in my opinion, idiocy) – repeating the same action over and over again and expecting different results. Or, as the Urban

Dictionary so eloquently puts it, "…doing the exact same freaking thing over and over again, expecting things to change." Spot on (insert clapping hands emoji here). It's quite simple actually, when you look at it this way.

So, if you've recognized that you're not truly happy with your life, and you know you need to take action to create change, then I revert back to my initial question – what is causing your unhappiness? Can you identify one key contributing factor, or are there multiple aspects that deep down you know you wish you could change? Do you even know what it would take to make you happy?

This part may actually prove to be much more of a challenge than taking that annoying step of admitting to yourself that you're unhappy in the first place. You'll need to identify your personal goals and life standards, so you know what it is you're striving towards. What will define your happiness, and how will you work to achieve it? Or perhaps the question should instead be what is causing your current unhappiness?

Long before Jack and I were married, I was in an intense romantic relationship. Like any couple, Dean and I had our highs and lows. We were best friends, talking all day and night. We truly loved and motivated one another. In fact, some of the best days of my life were spent with him. But all of that didn't change the fact that I called my friend Abby, crying with the same problems every week. Her response was a broken record.

"If you keep doing what you're doing, nothing is going to change. If you take some time away, things will either change or they won't…and then you'll have your answer."

I think the hardest part was that when I finally took Abby's advice and time away from the relationship, Dean didn't try to change anything at all. The saying "actions speak louder than words" proved heartbreakingly true. His actions were loud and clear. There was nothing left for me to do at this point except move forward without him. Not that I regret any of our time together because it is all part of my story and what got me to where I am today…but I waited five long years to get the answer I could have gotten in six months.

So why did I wait so long to face the harsh reality of ending my relationship with Dean? Because I was terrified to go through the pain of losing him, even though deep down I knew it would eventually end.

Every time I attempted to move on from our text messages, phone conversations and coffee dates, I would terribly miss his presence in my life and let him back in. I never actually allowed myself to experience and process the pain of losing him, so I kept "resetting my clock," forcing myself back to square one.

No doubt, the pain of moving on from something or someone you love hurts...A LOT. But the sooner you go through the pain and allow yourself to mourn the loss of this new void, the closer you are to your future happier self. Each time you make the decision to go back to something that you know in your heart is detrimental to your well-being, you're just setting yourself up to feel the pain of loss all over again...and pushing true personal fulfillment further away. Yes, the first few weeks, months and even years are going to be hard, but if you don't face them, they will never be behind you.

Dean helped teach me a difficult lesson: it's best to face your challenges sooner than later, because it means you're that much closer to your better days ahead.

Have you ever heard the advice "Eat your frog in the morning?" It comes from a Mark Twain quote – "Eat a live frog every morning, and nothing worse will happen to you the rest of the day." The idea is that if you tackle the thing you least want to do first, you'll have more enjoyable things to look forward to from there. It has become popular in sales trainings, motivational speaking and blogs on simplifying life and improving time management.

The anguish of letting Dean go was my "frog." It tasted awful going down, but now I'm onto experiencing the more enjoyable things that life has to offer...the things that I deserve. My life became a lot simpler once I became a little more selfish, prioritizing my happiness and refusing to repeat the mistake of NOT doing so.

My relationship with Dean also taught me that sometimes love just isn't enough. It can definitely put you on the road to a healthy relationship, and it can keep you tuned in to one other to some extent. But love, in itself, isn't always enough to get you where you want (and need) to go. The initial magnetic attraction, fiery passion and affectionate companionship of a romantic connection are all amazing to experience. But unfortunately, they don't always exist in parallel with both parties' long-term needs and desires.

We've all been there...experiencing that flip in your stomach at the start, when everything about the relationship is genuinely thrilling. This new energy (and sexual chemistry) that's exploded into your life propels you daily, very much like a drug. You're literally high on the newness and all of the exciting "firsts" – the first dinner date, first vacation together, first Christmas as a couple, the first "I love you."

We get so caught up in these warm and fuzzy feelings and the idea that this just might have the potential to be "it" – our soulmate, our fairy tale ending, our happily ever after. But so many of us tend to neglect some of our long-term wants and needs as the relationship progresses. Too often we begin to sacrifice vital pieces of ourselves – opinions, values, goals – for the sake of keeping the idea of that perfect ending alive. And we begin to lie to ourselves, insisting that something will miraculously change.

A close friend of mine recently ended a relationship with a man who didn't want more children or to get married. She has always known she wants to have children and a family, and she puts a lot of value in the concept of her life partner legally becoming her husband. The relationship lasted about a year, until their long-term wants and needs started to surface and create feelings of resentment and distrust. I wholeheartedly believe that they loved each other. However, based on their individual approaches to attaining true happiness, love in and of itself wasn't enough. Nothing was ever going to change that, no matter how many days they lived pretending they could make it work.

These are definitely the hardest relationships to leave because there is an emotional and mental connection that can keep two people bound longer than they should be. Making a long-term commitment when both parties aren't on the same page isn't just relationship suicide…it's also a complete sabotage of both individuals' personal happiness. It's more than likely that these underlying opposing issues will resurface and eventually become the downfall of the relationship altogether.

I'm not saying that compromise isn't an important component of any successful relationship. There is however, usually a short list of desires and needs that are non-negotiable parts of a life plan. And it's crucial that both people in the relationship have an understanding of what's on their partner's non-negotiable list, so they're set up for success. This helps both of you (and the relationship) naturally progress to enhance your mental and physical health.

If moving out-of-state away from your family and best friends will always be a hard "no," then doesn't it make sense for your significant other to learn this earlier than later? Otherwise, he just may reveal months into the relationship that his dream is to move across the country to Napa to open his own winery? Wait, wasn't that a Carrie and Big scenario in Sex and the City? Funny how these little pop culture anecdotes really do seem to shape our subconscious perceptions of reality.

I think in addition to openly discussing one another's non-negotiables, there's also a number of crucial (seemingly unlearned) life skills typically present in couples who successfully maintain a healthy relationship. And I believe that the need for these life skills applies in all relationships, not only the romantic ones.

Perhaps the most important is to be aware of your emotions and demonstrate the ability to clearly communicate them. I think this is one of the top dilemmas we face as a human race: the inability to directly communicate our true feelings to the right person or people.

How many times has a friend called you primarily to moan and groan about a problem they're having with someone else - their friend, husband or co-worker? And then, when you ask if they've broached the topic with the person in question, they embarrassingly admit they have not. I'd argue that this probably happens about 75% of the time, and frankly, it acts as toxic fuel, causing problems to grow larger than they should ever become.

Here's a crazy idea – how about you openly and truthfully communicate to the other party what's bothering you and why? This would eliminate third party involvement, gossip and feelings of betrayal when it inevitably gets back to the other person that you were talking shit.

Usually, once the problem is resolved, you end up wishing you never told anyone else in the first place, right? Raise your hand if you've ever regretted blabbing to your friends in the heat of the moment about a minor dilemma with your significant other after it's all blown over and been worked out? Did you really need to air out the dirty laundry of your husband's insensitive comment just because it was compounded by your annoying AF work day and dreadful evening commute? Ok, you can put your hands down now. No judgement. I'm human and have been there myself.

The point is, I imagine that this scenario plays out all too often. We let our emotions get the best of us and rant to a friend or two about another relationship's turmoil, as opposed to sensibly expressing our feelings to the person actually involved in the dilemma.

There are obviously times when venting to others to get feedback and support is crucial. But many times, we act far too quickly based on our raging emotions, deviously leading us to overreact to relatively small issues that could have been easily resolved with proper identification of emotion and simple communication skills.

Always take the time to reflect on how you're feeling to get to the root of the issue without jumping the gun, dialing that phone, firing off that text, posting that status or spewing trash talk to the nearest warm body. Acting hastily on fresh negative feelings towards others (or yourself) will likely lead you down a reckless path that ends with regret.

If and when you do make the mistake of causing a rift in a relationship by not effectively communicating your sentiments to the right person the first time around, recognize it, own it, and learn from it. Don't keep making that same mistake over and over again because #1 – by definition, that makes you insane. And #2 – you will eventually find yourself lacking in quality relationships with others.

I think proactive and honest communication is highly underrated in today's world, whether coming from the President of our country, a coworker or a childhood friend. Be intelligent and mature enough to own your feelings and opinions, and deliver them in a sensible and diplomatic way. You may not always get it right, but if you have the courage to admit your mistakes, learn and move forward, you'll have a lot more success in love, friendship, business and even helping organize your kid's PTA bake sale.

CHAPTER 8

FLIGHT SCHOOL

Sometimes you have to sacrifice your own happiness to benefit those you love.

I'm not a parent, but I can imagine times when it's difficult to let your children fly. I remember when I decided to study abroad in Australia during my junior year of college. My parents certainly supported my decision, but I knew they were also scared to let me travel across the globe with 30 hours of flight time between us. Of course they wanted me to see the world and experience things they never had the opportunity to. They were thrilled for me, yes. But they were also naturally depressed being unable to see me for six months, and they knew they'd battle that signature parent anxiety each day wondering if I was ok. Remember, this was all taking place in "ancient times" before smart phones, tablets and facetime.

Nonetheless, they selflessly put their feelings aside, allowing me to live out my dreams. I'll never forget that and will always genuinely appreciate their sacrifice. Furthermore, their selflessness inspired me to look forward to a time in my life when I would be given the opportunity to do the same for someone else. And that opportunity came much sooner than I anticipated.

After returning from Australia, I registered for fall courses in my final year at Providence College. One of these classes was notoriously controversial across campus, hardly fitting the Jesuit institution's status quo. *The Sociology of Fertility*, more commonly known among students (and even faculty) as "the sex class," included lectures, discussion topics and assigned reading material that were always rather liberal, and even downright outrageous at times.

The professor openly addressed everything, and he expected us to do the same. There were plenty of days I could feel my face getting hot during group discussions. One of the more memorable of those days was when I listened to another student openly discuss having anal sex with his girlfriend. Although a bit scandalous, there was something about that class that made me feel more confident about my sexuality and more open to the idea of "awkward" conversations.

I was also lucky enough to make a great (and unexpected) friend in that class. Dillon was quiet, handsome and always had a shit-eating grin on his face begging you to ask the reason behind it. He had some kind of eternal mischievous secret behind those dark brown eyes.

As you can imagine, Dillon and I had some quite intimate conservations due to the nature of the class. He was far from my "type" (or so I thought), but I enjoyed his company and could tell him anything. I looked forward to seeing him walk into the classroom with the hood of his bulky black sweatshirt pulled up over his head, headphones on, stomping in his pristine suede work boots. In my opinion, he was a little "gangster," and far from the typical Providence College male. But he was unique.

He definitely didn't try to fit in, and I loved that about him.

One afternoon, Dillon and I were taking a ride off-campus to do some errands and grab a bite to eat. As we stepped out of the car, he suddenly snatched the pocketbook out of my hands and started doing his best impression of a casual feminine strut down the street with it flung over one arm. I found this unexpected glimpse into his rarely silly side absolutely hysterical. Dillon's demeanor was typically pretty serious, and he could even be described as shy. For the first time, I found myself attracted to him. It caught me completely off guard, and is actually pretty ironic when you think about it. A man carrying a purse turns me on?!

From that day on, we spent time together almost every day, which eventually led to a romantic relationship. When we graduated, we began our separate adult lives living in different towns, but continued to see each other every weekend.

Dillon helped move me into my very first apartment, which I shared with Abby. He gladly assembled all of my IKEA furniture, and always ensured that I had the coolest new technology. He loved to spoil me and make me feel special, although he was never the type to openly communicate or physically show it. I somehow just understood this was his way of showing affection.

Although Dillon and I showed affection in different ways, I learned through him that there are several languages of love, and you can't expect everyone to love exactly the same way you do. I think it's natural to seek a partner who loves the way you can best comprehend, but if you can open your heart and mind and learn to understand how others express their love, you'll find that there is so much more of it to be received in this world.

I've found this true in friendships as well. Not one of my girlfriends shows their love and loyalty exactly the same as the next. None of them offer identical friendship dynamics.

Abby is like the other side of my brain. I can call her any time of day to dissect a thought in my head, and she will always genuinely listen. Corinne is my trendy, social butterfly fashionista, always there to weigh in on the latest trends and lend her experience in digital advertising to advise on marketing and social media strategies for my latest business venture. And Chelsea is the practical rule follower, with whom I grew up, played soccer and attended college...someone who is always going to tell me exactly what I need to hear and correct my grammar while she does it...someone perfect for editing my life story!

Just like my closest girlfriends who offer a wide array of charisma and connections, Dillon had his own way of showing me how deeply he cared for me.

As he and I made our way into the real world, I took my very first sales role, and he began his journey pursuing a position with the United States Government. I knew from the start that his lifelong dream could mean his relocation to anywhere in the country. At the time, I secretly didn't want him to apply, but it was all he had talked about since the day we met in sex class. He loved criminology and was fascinated by the psychology of the human mind. We spent hours going through the application process and then months waiting to hear back.

Then it happened. There was an opening in southern California on the U.S. Border Patrol, and they wanted him for the job. That day can only be described as bittersweet. I was intensely proud and happy for Dillon to begin living his dream, but it meant months of training and moving across the country.

I never once made him feel guilty or tried to hold him back from doing what he had set out to do. The same way my parents had supported my semester abroad in Australia knowing they would miss me, I needed to support him going to California…without me.

The days between him opening the offer letter and leaving for the West Coast were miserable. I know I'm being dramatic, but it felt like he'd been diagnosed with stage four cancer and I was just waiting for him to die. We aggravated each other. We fought. And naturally, we pushed each other away. I think that's normal when you can't mentally handle the pain of disconnecting. It was the same way I fought with my parents the entire summer before I went off to college. It made it easier to leave.

When the day finally came for Dillon to fly out, it was worse than I could've imagined. For the first time I saw him cry. I cried. We hugged each other tightly, knowing it would never be the same.

We stayed in touch, and I visited him for Thanksgiving that year, but there was no denying that things were different. Our lives had changed, and so had we. The carefree days of college life were much different than taking on real life together. We chased very different dreams, and our paths were inevitably headed in different directions.

To this day, I have zero regrets that I encouraged Dillon to follow his dreams, even though they didn't involve me. We still keep in touch a few times a year about fitness, work and life, and he recently confided in me that our experience was the only time anyone had ever made that kind of sacrifice for him.

He texted, "I remember the day I left for Cali and you came by the house...I def appreciated how you handled it and let me go. I haven't had that experience since. People always want to hold on too tight, even at the expense of other people's lives."

I found myself smiling as I read his message. We undoubtedly crossed paths for a reason, and we both learned so much...both about our college classmates' sex lives and navigating life in general. What we had together just wasn't meant to be forever, and I'm ok with that.

CHAPTER 9

STEEL BARS

Don't be angry and resentful just because others encourage you to be.

My life is a soap opera. And the show isn't even close to over. Rewind back to 2008, when my father was sentenced to prison just a few years before my brother's passing. Visiting my dad "inside" just days after Bobby's death easily goes down as one of the worst in my life.

His steel blue eyes met mine from across the visiting room, tears streaming down his face. He began to sob violently. This was first time I'd ever seen my father openly cry. The pain in his eyes was that of someone brutally scarred by war, living to tell the story…although I think this was far worse for him. I don't think he wanted to live through the pain while his only son was no longer with us.

I know you're all dying to know what he did to land himself in the slammer, but we'll save that for another book. I will tell you that many people wanted me to hate my father for it. They wanted me to write him off like a restaurant receipt.

"Do you still speak to your dad?" they would ask in a disgusted, condescending tone. Apparently I was supposed to reply with something really shitty about him, followed

with an assertive "no." But, I didn't. I couldn't.
I loved my dad.

I definitely didn't (and never will)
approve of his behavior. Being utterly disgusted
by his choices is an understatement. But the
more people interrogated me, the more I found
myself breeding anger that I'm not sure even
existed when I initially learned of the crimes he
committed.

I let others get inside my head. I became
accustomed to feeling angry without even
realizing it (or why). I'm not sure when it all
really clicked for me, but thankfully one day it
did.

What about all of the great times I had with my father growing up? Maybe if he'd been a terrible father, I could have disowned him. But the fact of the matter is, he wasn't. My dad was very supportive of my goals and dreams. He was a huge part of my life in so many ways, and I couldn't be more grateful for my upbringing. He attended every single awards ceremony and soccer game. Because of his help, I always had one of the best science fair projects. He sat down at the dinner table to eat with us as a family every night and asked how my day was. He spent hours of his time driving me to tournaments and college visits. In short, he supported me in anything and everything I ever did. He loved me unconditionally and provided the best life he could for Bobby and me.

I had very few friends who grew up as lucky as I did, spending that much quality time with their parents, and I was grateful. My dad loved being a parent, and he knew the day I stepped foot onto my college campus that he'd raised me to be a self-sufficient woman that he could let fly.

As I began to reflect on my life and my father's place in it, I realized that any anger I was feeling towards him was, oddly enough, fueled mainly by other people. How had I not seen this earlier? And furthermore, how had I not realized that I was putting myself at a huge disadvantage by allowing it? It didn't hurt anyone except me to harbor this resentment. Only I was being brought down – imprisoned by this negative energy.

From that moment on, my outlook shifted completely. Why shouldn't my feelings towards my father be defined by OUR relationship and all the great years spent together? I can certainly be disappointed in him and disapprove of a handful of his actions, but why do I have to hate him? People make mistakes, and he is human like all of us.

Everyone is entitled to their own feelings and opinions, of course. However, I don't have to adopt them. It's not productive to live the rest of my life hating my father, when 99% of my time with him was positive. I choose to remember the joy my dad brought to my life, and I will always love him for that.

I can tell you firsthand that focusing on the positive instead of consciously working to preserve the negative is infinitely more healthy and beneficial to my mental state. Carrying anger or resentment from time to time is definitely a normal part of human emotion, but learning how to recognize and re-channel it is super important.

Be fair. Give yourself time to grieve and feel the anger (or other negative feelings that are warranted in any hurtful situation). But then, truly make the effort to allow compassion to overthrow your scorn. Try to shift your perspective and put yourself in the other person's shoes. Take the time to consider *why* they did what they did. Most of us are not deliberately evil; many are just selfish or think they won't suffer consequences. You will find more times than not that their intent was never to hurt anyone.

The next and very important step in releasing anger and resentment is to forgive. To be clear, forgiveness does not mean you're accepting the other person's harmful actions. It means you're letting go of anger that would otherwise hinder your emotional healing. It gives you the ability to move on and not live in the past. Or in my case, it allowed me the luxury of doing just that…living in the past, cherishing the fond memories I'd built with my father – the love and support he never failed to offer for years outside of the mistakes he made that lead him to break the law.

CHAPTER 10

ANOTHER REALM

You have the ability to do anything.

Have you ever taken the time to stop and consider how amazing human beings truly are? The potential we have? Every day I look around, and it's an understatement to say that the accomplishments of the human race are astonishing.

Take Mark Zuckerberg, for example. He developed Facebook – a word and concept that meant nothing to any of us prior to 2005. We all have the potential to create a phenomenon that has never before existed, and that's pretty damn amazing.

But many of us have a hard time pushing our brain into this realm – to comprehend and accept that anything is possible and there are no limits except those we impose on ourselves. In this realm, your potential is endless, and you can do or create just about anything you want. Whether through meditation, weightlifting, walking the beach or reading this book - if you can allow your mind to venture into this realm even once, you'll begin to understand what I mean.

My journey there took place with the creation of YourGymGF. Although our app didn't turn out as planned and our fitness brand doesn't even begin to compare to the monumental impact of Facebook, these are still things that never existed until Sonya and I created them.

I remember when the first horrible version of the mobile app was released, and I'd smile to myself overhearing women at the gym chirping excitedly about it as I went through my workout routine - "Have you downloaded YourGymGF yet?!" And when the first tank top order came in, everyone was so eager and proud to represent the brand. These moments brought me indescribable feelings of accomplishment and pride, making me want to bottle them up to be shared with the world. It just felt way too unfair to keep this wonderful experience all to myself.

It's exhilarating when a simple idea comes to fruition like that...especially when it's yours. It taught me that through visualization of goals and hard work, I can bring anything to life. Now my brain will forever reside in this new realm. I think once you transition, you won't ever go back because the drive to create and discover the unknown is just too fucking invigorating. It's a new way of thinking...a new way of life.

And when something or someone inspires you to "cross over" like that, I admit it's challenging to avoid becoming that overly enthusiastic person who can't stop smiling, talking about it, shouting from the rooftops wanting to get others on board to enjoy the sensation. I'm sure plenty of people out there secretly roll their eyes or get a bit overwhelmed when they hear someone like me promote my passions and this powerful feeling of creation and inspiration. Yes, there's one important truth to be told in all of this. It's definitely not easy to get here. In fact, it's so difficult that many people will criticize it, and most won't ever even try.

Well, I'm personally challenging you to take a stab at it. I'm challenging you to test your limits. Push yourself into a space you've never gone before, and for the love of God, don't do it for anyone else but yourself. Try something you've always been a little too scared to try. Create something you've always secretly contemplated but ultimately been dissuaded by that little dickhead voice of doubt in your head asking "But what if you fail?"

You've got to commit yourself to living right on the edge of your potential. Adjust your mind to feel comfortable with the concept of failing. Failure holds the key to an infinite space of your unlocked potential. Focus on the necessary actions that allow you to meet your goals. Fail fast to learn what not to do. Failure is where change occurs. Failure is where you start adapting. The people who have the hardest time pushing forward are those afraid to fail. Successful people fail. They fail often, and they fail over and over again. Failure will teach you, but it will never beat you if your determination to succeed is stronger than your will to quit. Failure defeats losers, but it inspires winners.

So, allow your brain to venture into a new space where you're the only leader of your life and only you determine your outcomes. All too often, we get so engulfed in the daily grind, the bills that need to be paid and the expectations of the (mostly boring) herd that we lose sight of the incredible visions we once had.

Maybe you've always wanted to go back to school and finish your degree. Maybe you want to get a totally different degree. Maybe you want to open your own bed and breakfast. Maybe you're dying to take a painting class, learn to remodel your own bathroom or participate in amateur night at a strip club! I don't care how you conceptualize your goals of doing and creating...but I do care that you are doing yourself a disservice by NOT doing and creating.

Every single day when you get out of bed, you have a choice. Some days it's not going to be as easy as others. I know just as well as anyone that life can and will certainly test your willpower with a lot of adversity. You must find your purpose in each day and choose strength as the only option. If you see yourself as weak, then weak you will be. If you really want to be strong, accomplished and personally fulfilled, your actions must directly reflect that drive.

Although those of us who've already made it over to this realm may sometimes come off annoyingly positive or a bit preachy, it's only because we know what you're missing out on by not being over here with us just yet. I promise it's way more fun on this side of the things. Push yourself to realize your true abilities, and please join us sooner than later!

Maybe we can use Zuckerberg's phenomenon and create a Facebook group (wink wink).

CHAPTER 11

GRABBING THE BULL(SHIT) BY THE HORNS

Hold yourself accountable, but stay realistic with your goals.

Do you ever lie to yourself? Swear up and down that you're going to do something new or productive and then just don't ever get around to it? Of course you do. We're all guilty of this at one time or another. But frankly, we all need to cut the crap and start having more respect for ourselves.

How long has it been since you moved into your "new" house? And that mound of boxes still standing in the corner of your basement untouched? Stop pretending it's going to take you ages to sift through these "essential" belongings to get organized. Let's be honest. You know deep inside that if you've gone this long without using the contents of those boxes, then you can likely get rid of almost everything inside without missing it. And your ancient clothes or household knick-knacks may be worn-out junk to you, but there are so many less fortunate people who'd be elated to receive those hand-me-down treasures. Make the time (realistically a mere hour out of your weekend) to clear that pesky pile. You'll be pleasantly surprised at how great it feels to cross it off your list, and you'll feel even better after making a car trunk load of donations to Goodwill or your local church.

To take my hypothetical self-improvement scenarios a step further, how many times have you looked in that dreaded full-length mirror hating what you see staring back at you? You've made countless vows to start eating heathier and follow a regular workout routine, but you just can't seem to find the motivation to make it a reality.

Putting in long days at work, raising kids, running countless errands and trying to fit time into the day to read a chapter of a book or watch your favorite Netflix show are all very real priorities to balance. And unfortunately, they can easily become excuses used to justify why you "just don't have time in the day" to cook a healthy meal or take that weekly spin class you always see your friends posting about on Facebook.

Well I call bullshit. Nowadays, we have endless options available right at our fingertips via the internet, social media, apps and tons of other amazing resources. You literally have no excuse to stay in that mirror-loathing rut. Rut rimes with gut. Nobody wants either. So, get your ass in gear, start telling yourself some truth, build some muscle and cut some inches off that waste line. Do a little online research, hit the grocery store for healthy ingredients, spend some time meal-prepping once a week and commit to a realistic fitness routine that fits your lifestyle so it will work.

Even if you're low on funds, time or not sure where to begin, you can quickly surf the web to find a plethora of easy clean eating recipes that won't break the bank, along with some simple, free at-home workout routine videos available on YouTube. And now there's even an entire industry of grocery/meal delivery services like Amazon, PeaPod and HelloFresh. Some of these companies focus primarily on ingredients that fit a healthy lifestyle, organic eating or other dietary restrictions. Sorry, but you really have no excuses left to lie to yourself about being unable to commit to a better you.

And get that untrue notion out of your head that you have to start with huge, intimidating goals in order to alter your life. Make them more realistic, and they instantly become more attainable. Adjusting things slightly does not mean giving up...it means setting yourself up to win.

For example, I recognized that during a busy week of work appointments, I was typically making it to the gym for an effective workout three days on average. So, I began to make real calendar appointments with MYSELF for three of the seven days, and committed to an attainable plan. Instead of telling myself I was going to work out every single day or spend several hours at a time grinding away at the gym, I made a practical promise to show up and work really hard for 45-60 minutes for those three time slots. This more realistic promise to myself allowed me to actually keep it! And at the end of each week, I was able to give myself a celebratory (albeit imaginary) high-five for the accomplishment of meeting my physical activity goals.

It becomes pretty simple. Being proud and feeling accomplished is so much more enjoyable than closing out your week beating yourself up because you pretended you were going to follow an Olympic athlete's training plan and failed miserably to hold yourself to it. And seeing real results from your workouts means more than just showing up so can say you walked into the building. It means moving, sweating, breathing heavily and putting in genuine effort for the time you're there. So, ditch the texting and Instagramming, switch your smartphone to your dance cardio streaming music station, and get in the zone.

In addition to mapping out an achievable workout regimen, I also adjusted my eating habits to create a better balance for my body from the inside out (more on that later). My point is, it feels fabulous when you commit to something and follow through with it, especially when it's something that brings more positive energy, confidence, structure and commendation (from both others and yourself).

Alternatively, it feels pretty shitty when you don't follow through on the things you claim to be committed to. You end up feeling lazy, like a disappointment to the most important person in your life...you! How are you going to stay motivated, find success and achieve real happiness by constantly disappointing yourself? Reality check: you're not.

If you don't like to be lied to by others, then why make it acceptable to lie to yourself?

It breeds stagnancy and unhappiness. Hold yourself to a higher standard, and follow through on the things you say you'll do, whether it's taking the trash out regularly or booking that volunteer trip to South Africa you've talked about for years.

I promise you'll be pleasantly surprised by the results, and this follow-through mentality will inherently create life habits that fuel new energy, productivity and a positive lifestyle. Your drive for success will increase the more you produce. I swear the more you achieve the more motivated you become. Accountability and the realization of your goals is blissfully addictive.

CHAPTER 12

SPINNING STRAW

Keep yourself off the proverbial pity pot.

If my life sounds like it can be a little complicated at times, well that's because it can. My dad went to prison, my brother died in a car accident and my mom was diagnosed with breast cancer - all within a pretty short period.

It would've been easy for anyone in my situation to fall into a dismal spiral of sadness and sit around feeling sorry for themselves. But rather than dwell in the "Why me?" state-of-mind in its most common negative context, I chose to ask "Why me?" in a curiously optimistic way. I chose to examine the possibility that my unfavorable circumstances may have arrived with a greater purpose and an ironically positive intent. Approaching things in this way has helped me grow more than I ever imagined possible.

Yes, these tragedies were initially crippling, but they somehow created a magnifying glass focused squarely on my emotions, values and who I was at my core. Instead of obsessing over what I'd lost, I gave some serious thought to what I still have to be grateful for. Basically, the value of what I had (and still have) sky-rocketed after being faced with such adversity.

It's similar to the saying "You don't know what you've got until it's gone." Except in my case, the suffering and loss highlighted all of the amazing things I was lucky enough to have still inside of myself, my family, friends, experiences and my ability to wake up every day making the choice to live my best life. I truly enjoy life more than I ever did before these tragic events took place because I've learned to feel intense gratitude for all of my blessings, knowing they may not last forever.

Consciously choosing to live in this perpetually grateful state of mind allows me to love more deeply, laugh more often, take bigger risks and simply exist more freely in mind, body and soul. I choose to believe that my heartache serendipitously put me on a path towards some of the happiest days of my life.

Pretty cool, huh? I can transform a pity pot into a pot of gold. Just call me Rumpelstiltskin.

And guess what? You have the ability to do this in your life too! Anyone can do it. It's all about attitude.

I don't want to sound insensitive, but you need to know that somebody somewhere always has it much worse than you do, no matter what you're going through. Yes, it's hugely disappointing that you didn't get the work promotion you'd hoped for, but you still have a solid paycheck coming in, allowing you to feed your family and put a roof over your heads. The guy panhandling at the end of the off-ramp that you pass every weekday driving to use your (rather pricey) monthly gym membership can't say the same. When you're feeling frustrated and hopeless, remind yourself of your blessings, and practice some mindful gratitude.

I remember a time at my pharmaceutical sales job when I was hugely aggravated by a new company initiative that I saw as a complete waste of time. I found myself driving around miserably for a good portion of the day, answering calls from coworkers who shared my feelings.

But I quickly snapped out of it, recognizing how stupid I was acting and that my conversations with the other reps were only perpetuating my negative mood and aggravation. If I had to drive around in a company car for a few weeks, get paid great money and drop off booklets to each of my accounts (whose business kept me able to pay my bills), then my life really wasn't that bad at all.

It sure wasn't what I wanted to be doing with my time, but then again, I wasn't the CEO of the company. Sometimes you have to shut up, slap a smile on your face, take your marching orders, play your cards and make the most of your situation, even if it's not ideal. I also vowed from that point on that in times when negative work gossip was running rampant, I'd make the decision not to partake. Staying positive and working hard was much more productive and fulfilling than spending a day bashing the company.

Sometimes, when I'm starting to feel aggravated with work, I'll even call my manager just to list off all of the things I'm grateful for at our company. It helps realign my focus and keep me grounded when I'm on the brink of whining or focusing on the negative stuff that's pretty trivial in the grand scheme of things.

You can and will find things to be grateful for each day, whether you choose to say them inside your head or actually recite a list out loud. It can be as simple as your home, where you live, your job, family or health. And it can be more high-level like being in shape or possessing self-confidence.

My point is there's something positive to find in any day or situation. But if you plop down and spend all of your time throwing yourself a pity party, you won't have any time and energy left to find that gold lining (screw, silver…I'm aiming for the best)!

CHAPTER 13

A SECOND FIRST IMPRESSION

You create your own reality, including others' perception of you.

I can't think of a better way to describe myself as a high school freshman than "legs with a backpack" - a backpack that always seemed larger than my body. I could never be sure when I was going to get an extra minute to do some homework, so every single binder and textbook was on my back, literally weighing me down at all times.

My (still prepubescent) physique was a bit of an anomaly – a short square torso, long thin gazelle legs and chubby chipmunk cheeks that hadn't changed since my grade school days. It wouldn't have made a difference if I shaved my legs or not. But I was 14, and that's what 14-year-old girls did, right?

The other girls also wore spaghetti strap dresses to the annual Homecoming dance. I, on the other hand, wore a short-sleeved velour dress from the kids' department of Filene's (with no need for a bra). Yes, velour...from the KIDS' department.

I was an athlete, a member of the Student Council, National Honor Society and graduated tenth in my class out of over 330 students...and all of that wasn't enough. I wanted to be a spaghetti strap girl…but I was too scared to make out with boys on the dance floor, terrified to speak up for myself and teased because I had zero interest in ripping shots (and puking up) burning concoctions stolen from our parents' liquor cabinets. I was innocent, sweet and terrified to do anything that might sabotage next week's Applebee's dinner date with my parents.

I guess inviting the rest of the girls' soccer team over for a winter hot tub night just didn't cut it, unless it included boners and "bee-ahs" (that's beers for those outside of New England; for some reason, we drop the letter "r" where it belongs and add it where it doesn't).

No matter how hard I tried to show my peers that I was a fun-loving, normal teen with a good heart who could fit into their cool world, I was always left feeling the same - unaccepted and disappointed. Nobody dreaded the Monday morning weekend recap conversations in first period more than I did.

"Kate hooked up with Mike at Jim's party Saturday night - she's so hot."

What did hooking up even mean? Did he touch her boobs? Stick his tongue down her throat? Or did they go all the way? Hopefully not, because she could get pregnant...or an STD...or something, right? Plus, that would've been kind of slutty since Mike isn't her boyfriend. I mean, that's what my dad told me.

I wish I could travel back in time and shake some sense into those legs with a backpack. I may have been a book smart straight-A student, but I was still young and totally unsure of myself, making me act pretty darn stupid a lot of the time. I somehow didn't see that I could be a spaghetti strap girl, even dead sober in my short-sleeved velour dress, if I had just decided to go ahead and be one. It was as simple as that.

Thank God for Abby, or I'd probably still be getting off the bus crying once a week. Of course, I'm not riding the school bus nowadays, but you know what I mean. I met Abby exactly when I was supposed to…in Spanish class that first year of high school. She sat directly in front of me and used to walk in holding her blonde head high, with one book (if that), a stylish handbag and some sort of chewy candy in hand. She'd sit and chomp her way through class, seemingly without a care in the world. And when test time came, she knew where to get her answers. Side note: my Spanish vocabulary is still off the hook to this day.

I didn't even care that she cheated off of me because Abby was awesome. Although she was definitely one of the "hot" girls, with her long blonde hair and striking face that could be on a magazine cover, she was quite humble (and still is to this day). She was by far the most unassuming high school girl I'd ever met.

She was genuine - not the type that would talk to you in class and then pretend she didn't know you in front of a different crowd in the hallways. She was always just Abby. To her, high school was like a Friday night stroll through the mall with friends. Nothing fazed her, not even a final exam. We couldn't have been more opposite.

By the end of senior year, we'd become great friends. We did everything together that summer before college - graduation parties, concerts, beach days on the Cape - you name it. And we had a blast no matter what we got into.

One of the things I've always loved most about Abby is that considering what other people might think about her is a foreign concept. She can't even comprehend it, which is probably why she even hung out with me in the first place. She absolutely owns who she is.

I'm not sure exactly when I realized it, but at some point it hit me that Abby had found a way to define how other people viewed her. She could do some crazy shit, and nobody would say a word about it. Even teachers and other adults seemed to be absorbed in her trance. In fact, I think most people actually admired her for her nonchalance and spontaneity.

Her free spirit and thirst for life was undeniably contagious. She'd go after things that seemed so out of reach at our age, and more often than not, she was successful. And if she wasn't, she didn't dwell on it...onto the next adventure! She landed herself a job as a cocktail waitress at the busiest bar in town, and I don't think she was even eighteen. I was in awe that nothing seemed to scare her, and nothing could change her own confident perception of herself. She was always just Abby, Abby, Abby.

That summer before college was one of the best of my life. It was that summer (in large part thanks to Abby) that I began to meet the real Sarah. And Sarah was actually pretty damn cool. I realized I was funny, smart, caring, genuine, happy, positive and even kind of cute with my new, more mature look. The boys not only knew I existed, but they also wanted to hang out, take me on dates and see how far I'd let them go (if you know what I mean).

By the time I went off to college, I was ready to get the hell out of my hometown. I craved the opportunity to make first impressions all over again...to be unapologetically me. I blasted country music on the second floor of McVinney Hall (subwoofer and all), and I proudly introduced myself to my new floormates, even if their eyes squinted and lips pursed as they walked past my dorm room. I could tell they weren't huge fans of Nashville's Top Hits, but that didn't bother me one bit. I wasn't changing who I was. Not this country guurrrl! By the time we graduated, Kenny Chesney was a regular request on the pregame playlist.

Now at the age of 34, I find it insane that so many people, even those much older than I am, still allow others' opinions to shape how they view themselves and what they can or cannot do, say, feel, believe in, eat, spend their money on, listen to, agree with or deem valuable. I see it every day…in the workplace, at the gym, in social settings, politics and even in marriages.

Remember, it's just an OPINION. You have the choice to let someone else's become your reality, or you can choose your own...like Abby and I have.

Believe it or not, others will respect you for sticking to your guns and owning who you are. It may be slightly subconscious in our society, considering most of us have in some way been made to feel like we should "fit in" with the rest of the crowd since childhood. However, that admiration that Abby seemed to gain by just being herself was real. There's no doubt that people gravitate to that kind of quiet confidence.

I'll probably always face some kind of pressure to let others dictate my sense of truth and who I am at my core. But I've learned that I owe it to myself to not only maintain and reveal the authentic me, but to also truly love what makes me who I am. And when I love me, I've learned others will follow my lead.

CHAPTER 14

KNITTING A BLANKET

Vulnerability creates the strongest bonds.

Over fifteen years have passed, and Abby and I are still the best of friends. We talk about everything...and I mean everything! A recent phone conversation for instance, explored her difficulties walking after sex...

"I'm just always sore because it's so thick!" Shall I go further?

I softly chuckled, partly because of her blatant honesty, but more so because I was on the Stair Master at the gym, and she was on speaker phone. I glanced around to make sure nobody else was listening.

It's not the classiest of conversations, and if I'm being honest, they almost never are. I'm certain that on any given day, we sound like two dirty old country western dudes sitting in a saloon, instead of two young ladies. But it's not always about sex. Plenty of our girl talk lands on much less juicy topics, like our own individual quirks.

"I have a confession. I make Jack lint roll his feet every night before getting into bed because the dog hair gives me constant anxiety."

"I was driving home from the bar last night and had to pop a squat (not at the gym…at the post office). I couldn't hold it, so I pulled over, hiked up my sundress and went for it behind a dumpster."

There's no personal thought or act that I think twice about sharing with Abby. We're so mentally in tune that I often think she may know me better than I know myself. She can finish my sentence or put into words a thought I wasn't even fully aware I was thinking. And I know without a doubt that she would never judge me, even if she didn't necessarily agree with me. My mom constantly reminds me how lucky I am to have a friend like Abby. She affectionately repeats for the millionth time that most people will never have the chance to experience that level of friendship in their lifetime.

But I think it's more than just luck that allowed us to build such a bond. You see, I've learned that beautiful friendships are achieved when two people, over time, consciously decide to be completely vulnerable with each other.

Vulnerability is often confused with weakness or lacking the ability to defend yourself. However, it's quite the opposite to me. I see it as the key to building a strong foundation for trust and respect between two people - a foundation that's defined by lines of open communication, honesty and non-judgmental attitudes.

It isn't always easy to be vulnerable. In fact, for most people it probably doesn't come naturally, since it brings with it the huge emotional risk of being let down, laughed at or insulted. Letting yourself be vulnerable means being completely transparent in your thoughts, views, quirks, mistakes and shortcomings, while embracing those of others.

For you it may be drinking coffee naked on a conference call when your romantic partner arrives home. For someone else it means divulging a sexy dream to a friend. And for another it may be as simple as admitting they cried when their family dog passed away. Although it looks and sounds different from one person to the next, it's all the same concept - exposing yourself emotionally, which ultimately leads to deeper connections.

With how many people in your life can you say that you're truly that emotionally candid? Not many? Why?? I promise you're missing out on some pretty remarkable relationships.

Rather than trying to shield yourself for fear of what others might see, try embracing and sharing the "raw" you – the special parts that make you who you are (the laughs, the tears and the embarrassing moments). When you stop trying to impress people with a specific demeanor or a cinematic version of yourself, the gateway to ultimate connections is paved. I think these are the only kind of relationships worth building. Otherwise, aren't you just acting your way through life, blindly guessing at what version of yourself you think the world wants to see?

I think we'd all be much happier dropping the act because there are people out there who will enjoy the real, vulnerable you. There's infinite contentment in just curling up in your own skin and hanging out. And when you find someone who can hang right there with you, that's someone worth holding onto.

I've found that the relationships in which I'm most vulnerable have transformed into the coziest of security blankets. At 34 years old, I have so many amazing thriving friendships, and vulnerability is a major factor in all of them on a daily basis. You should try it.

CHAPTER 15

CAMPAIGN MANAGER

Be your own advocate. Nobody else is going to do it for you.

A year after my brother passed away, my mom was diagnosed with triple negative breast cancer - a more rare and aggressive form. Let me share a little bit about how SHE discovered it.

First, it's important to understand that my mother is an absolute fitness fanatic and has a better body than I do. She can see striations in almost every muscle. She's strong. She's healthy. She's definitely not someone you would even think to associate with "the C word." But we all know cancer doesn't discriminate. And with Bobby's passing, she wasn't sleeping, eating or managing her stress. I can't emphasize enough how much we as a society underestimate how essential these factors are to our health.

Anyway, back to detecting the cancer. My mom had mentioned to me in a few separate conversations that she kept feeling a "zing" sensation traveling from her armpit to nipple. She initially thought it could be from her weight training at the gym, but the sensation didn't subside. She had just had a mammogram, and nothing was red flagged. But still, she just didn't feel right about it.

She made an appointment with her primary care physician to discuss the sensation, and she specifically requested a proactive ultrasound for peace of mind. Sure enough, there was a mass the size of a pebble just in front of her pectoral muscle. It was biopsied immediately, and shortly thereafter, I received a hysterical phone call. "Sarah...Sarah, I have cancer!"

She couldn't believe it, and neither could I. Not only did she have breast cancer, but the prognosis for triple negative wasn't very optimistic. The doctors predict that if she hadn't advocated for herself, she probably would've been dead within five years.

Because my mom pushed to detect her cancer (and likely due to her already health-conscious lifestyle), she has beaten the odds. She is now healthy - back to a demanding workout schedule and exceptionally clean diet to combat its return.

This one is short and sweet. You know yourself better than anyone. If your gut is telling you something (in any situation), follow it. Whether it relates to your health, your love life, your family, your career or something as seemingly insignificant as insisting that the nail technician trim your nails shorter than she freakin' wants to, it's your responsibility to lead your own campaign! You only live once, and everyone else is too busy living their own lives and putting their asses first to worry too much about yours.

Yes, there are "experts" out there to help guide you in certain situations. But doctors, teachers and (dare I say it?) even your parents are all human. They don't know everything. They make mistakes. They don't have a crystal ball to tell you what choices will ultimately be best for you. And they can't possibly be as in tune with your mind, body and soul as you are.

Disclaimer: I'm absolutely not telling you to ignore good advice from the educated and experienced folks who love and care for you. Your dentist is probably right that you should be flossing more regularly, and your mother can offer some helpful tips on how to get your first baby to latch when breastfeeding.

But remember that the voice inside your head is the most intuitive. You can almost always rely on it to put your best interest first, survive and thrive. And don't stop at just listening to that internal voice. Use it to project your real and audible voice when necessary. If you're sitting around waiting for someone else to speak up on your behalf, you're wasting your time. You're the best advocate for you, and it's a powerful thing to realize and put into practice.

It may even save your life.

CHAPTER 16

THE POWER OF PRESENCE

Be there to support someone, even if you can't fix the problem.

There we were. A year past my brother's death, with a whole new daunting mountain to climb. I remained strong and positive in front of my mother, but the thought of losing her to cancer terrified me. Bobby was gone, my father was in prison, and now my mom? That's my entire family. I wasn't even thirty years old.

We made the decision to have her treated at Dana-Farber Cancer Institute in Boston - one of the world's top oncology facilities. Treatment consisted of surgery to remove the mass, eight rounds of chemotherapy and 30 days of radiation. She'd lose all of her thick, black curly hair and feel sick more often than not, all while agonizing over the odds of her own survival. I knew she was even more scared than I was. Especially after everything we'd already been through, the primal force of protective motherly instincts fueled her terror (and anger) at fate for even considering taking her from me.

I was pissed off too. And determined as hell to do anything in my power to aid her recovery. However, in all reality, I had no choice but to simply be there to support her physically and (more importantly) emotionally, as she fought and waited on the results of treatment. It was one of the most difficult internal battles I've fought to this day.

I always forced myself to begin my visits with a big smile on my face. I'd summon my often-fake courage, walk in her front door and make my way to her cozy bedroom...but the second she saw me she'd start to cry. It was the most helpless I've ever felt. There was absolutely nothing I could do, and it was excruciating. I'd always been a "fixer" – there to help others talk things out, offer advice and try to make them feel better in some way. This time I was unable to do any of these things. I had to sit back and watch my mom be tormented physically, mentally and emotionally….as if she hadn't been through enough in the past year! I couldn't begin to imagine how she was feeling, but I knew I had to be strong, even if it meant sacrificing my own comfort.

So, I encouraged her to express her feelings, cry whenever she needed to and never feel one ounce of guilt about any of it. My favorite way to support her was by focusing on her daily wins, both big and small. This could mean walking to the mailbox or getting in a 20-minute workout in her home gym over the garage. I didn't let the cancer define the way I viewed her, and I made sure to keep her fully aware of that.

In hindsight, our shared indescribable fear of the unknown and exhausting battle against a virtually invisible enemy taught us more than we could've anticipated about our mother-daughter bond. We'd always loved each other unconditionally, but a threat this strong forced us to lean on each other in a way we had never known. I couldn't offer any medicine or ginger ale to make her bounce back like usual. But I could be present. I couldn't assure her everything was going to be ok because I had no idea if that was true. But I could voice my own fear of her mortality, and hope that it somehow made her feel like she wasn't alone in her agony.

It's something I'm not sure I can put into words...the feeling of subduing years of acquired logic telling you there's a solution to every problem. Perhaps if I just did some more research, fed her some new magical vitamins or took her to some sacred mountain in the Middle East, I could help save her. But ultimately, all I could do was be there to help facilitate her treatment by experts and offer emotional sustenance (as her only living child) when she needed it most.

In addition to her reclaimed health, the result was our relationship becoming infinitely stronger. And we even grew separately as individuals. We both realized that waking up tomorrow morning is not a given, and nobody can ever be a fixer of all things. There will be times in life when you can't possibly have all the answers or make someone feel better. But you can offer your support in other ways…ways that become more valuable in that moment than can ever be measured.

Who knows if my mom's treatment would've been as successful if she didn't have the support system she found in me? My guess is no. Yes, she needed the chemotherapy to fight her battle, but I believe she needed my unspoken support just as much.

If you have a friend or family member facing any of the infinitely possible life tragedies – physical or mental illness, loss of a loved one, miscarriage, fertility challenges, addiction, career hurdles, family or relationship struggles (the list goes on and on) – you'll find that no matter how hard you try to listen and help them improve their situation, these challenges are somewhat out of your hands. No matter how much you love them, there's no magic wand you can wave to take away their pain. The recipe for overcoming these obstacles is quite subjective, and will not produce results overnight. It's equal parts self-recognition, education, determination, tears, anger, venting, regression, progression, medicine, listening ears, shoulders on which to cry, hugs and fierce, undying love. Commit yourself to offering those you can from the list. You may not feel like it's enough, but it will do more good for your loved one than you'll ever know.

CHAPTER 17

MOMENTUM

Push yourself to your physical and mental limits, even (and especially) in hard times.

My mom swore from the start of treatment that she'd remain positive, healthy and strong throughout her journey. She made that promise to herself on the very day she was diagnosed. She knew she had a long road ahead, but she was as ready as possible to take it on. I remember the inspiration I felt looking into her eyes - seeing the drive of an Olympian crouching at the starting line, waiting for that gun shot to sound.

Then chemotherapy began. I witnessed it in a mind-boggling oxymoronic light. It was heaven and hell, a vicious poison that somehow had a chance to save her life. After just one round, my mom looked as if she'd lived on the streets for a year. She is one of the strongest women I know, and I found myself surprisingly unprepared for her to actually appear sick. Her skin became ghostly white, her eyes no longer sparkled and a deathly shadow had been cast upon her. Her hair began falling out, and her routine became spending the entire first post-chemo day in bed. She described feeling like she'd been hit by a new bus each time around.

By day three post-treatment, she would miraculously regain what she liked to call her little window of energy and opportunity. A true warrior, she'd tie a bandana onto her pale, bald head, pull on her hot pink t-shirt proudly displaying the word "FIGHT" and make her way up the stairs to her home gym. She somehow mustered the strength to walk or jog on the treadmill and do some mild weight training for her upper body in these self-motivated sessions. Some days she'd stay up there for only 15 minutes, and some two hours. She relished in the fact that she was able to take advantage of even the smallest amount of energy – the tiniest sliver of physical strength ignited her mentally to push herself beyond the expected limits, and then some.

Every single day of this war was different. Some were great, some were ok and some were just terrible. On those torturous days that felt like lost battles, she just couldn't make the climb up those stairs no matter how much she yearned for the validation of normalcy.

She learned not to allow herself any level of expectation when she awoke to face a new day. She did whatever she could in each moment, listened to her body and respected her limits. This made her feel positive and able to maintain some level of control, even when she was having a dark day. I loved seeing that twinkle in her eyes return when she was having a good day, and it inspires me that she never let fighting cancer define her values or the things she wanted to accomplish.

That year in the midst of treatment, on a dreary wet St. Patrick's Day morning, she showed up, a rainbow in various shades of green, in several layers of warm clothing and a cozy winter hat to run the local 5-kilometer road race. I could tell she was more tired running than ever before, and it was heartbreaking to see her struggle. My stomach twirled in knots, but I just kept beaming and bragging to everyone, proclaiming that she was my mom and how amazing she was. I had no choice but to fuel her strength by remaining supportive and upbeat, even if I was struggling inside. I owed it to her to be her unfailing cheerleader after watching her fight every day just to get out of bed, much less take on the challenge of this race. And I had the honor of watching her slowly jog across the finish line in her festive little outfit, not caring one bit about her time, even if she came in dead last out of all the runners. She was just proud to finish, and proud doesn't even begin to describe how I felt.

I'll never know what brought on my mother's cancer or understand the scientific ways her draining treatment managed to fight off this unwelcome intruder. The one thing I do believe without a doubt is that her overall attitude, drive and physical state of health played an enormous role in the outcome of the shitty hand she was dealt. Her strength (in every sense of the word) allowed her the ability to take her life back and maintain her sense of livelihood when it would have been so much easier to pack it in, stay in bed and feel sorry for herself. Today, cancer-free, this little Wonder Woman is back to running, cycling and crushing an active lifestyle.

My mom's battle taught me never to underestimate the power of movement. Even if you feel beaten down and don't know what challenge lurks around the next bend, keep going at your own pace, putting one foot in front of the other. Keep making moves to get yourself to a more positive place, even when you want to quit.

It's also important to recognize that tests of your will power will not always be presented in the form of an illness or physical challenge. Your vitality will be threatened by a number of intangible life circumstances, and you're the only person with the power to make the decision that your divorce, layoff, state championship loss or tenth editor rejection email will not define you.

It's only natural for these experiences to pull you down emotionally for a period of time.

You're supposed to feel those feelings of grief and disappointment...they're what make you human. But what makes you an exceptional human is the recognition that yes, this situation sucks...but nonetheless, you're going to do what may feel impossible at the moment. You're going to pick yourself up, dust yourself off and look the next challenging day straight in the eye and vow to it that you will do everything in your power to push through to a stronger state of being.

When you feel like you have nothing left to give, that's when you need to dig deeper and find the drive you don't even necessarily believe exists. You are so much stronger than you know, and you can only discover the depths of your stamina if you push your so-called limits. You'll thank yourself later when you're able to look back on the experience as a step towards a stronger you. You may even find yourself oddly appreciative because it helped you recognize that only you can define your limits, and that you'll now be armed with a greater sense of strength the next time you face adversity.

CHAPTER 18

CLEAN FUEL

Nutrition, nutrition, nutrition!

You know the feeling. You've had one hell of a work week. Everything that could've gone wrong did. You've barely controlled the profane word vomit you're dying to spew at your boss, and you almost put your fist through the computer. But the good news is that it's Friday evening, and you've made it to the light at the end of the nine to five tunnel…you deserve to reward yourself.

So, you walk in the door, make a beeline for the fridge, grab a beer and shuffle through

takeout menus to answer the age-old question –
pizza or Chinese?

We often think that crushing a pizza,
gorging on candy or slamming back ten beers
will make us happy. Rewarding ourselves with
this type of consumptive behavior may make us
feel better for a brief moment. But don't you
find the fleeting high soon replaced by feelings
of discontent, lethargy, regret or at the very least
a brutal stomach ache? Let me tell you from
years of experience in physical training, diet and
exercise that food is actually one of the most
powerful triggers of depression and anxiety.

Simply put, our bodies are machines,
requiring proper fuel to function efficiently.

Born from our caveman roots, we'll perform even the simplest activities much better and longer on wholesome ingredients rich in vitamins and nutrients. I know I sound like an episode of Sesame Street, but too many people tragically underestimate the significance of what they put into their bodies. I'm flabbergasted that a large majority of the population (at least in our country) seem to have developed this whacky ability to disconnect the concept of what's going into their mouth (on their skin, in their lungs, etc.) and how they feel, act and look.

Newsflash people! In this case, ignorance is most definitely NOT bliss. Poor nutrition has real consequences. Consuming excess sugar, preservatives and processed crap that we crave in our emotional eating moments will leave us crashing and burning. And I'm not just talking about developing a "dad bod" or muffin top. This kind of "fake" sustenance can rather quickly create a domino effect, wreaking havoc in more areas than one – physically, mentally and emotionally. We've seen all of the articles flying around social media recently. Well, I firmly believe they're true…everything starts in your gut!

Let me preface this by saying I'm a huge proponent of balance. You're setting yourself up to fail if you pretend you can eat strictly clean ingredients all day every day without falling off the wagon. Let's be realistic (refer back to Chapter 11). I eat nachos, love me some red wine and treat myself to an occasional ice cream cone on a steamy summer afternoon. I wouldn't be human if I didn't give into these indulgences every so often.

The simple trick that's worked wonders for me in resetting my mind and body is to go by the 80/20 rule. This means that I stick to consuming lean protein, vegetables, grains and healthy fats 80% of the time. The other 20% consists of the vices...probably 19% red wine if I'm being honest.

I've always been athletic and remained pretty active since my youth soccer days.

Looking at me now, a stranger would probably assume I've been obsessed with all things fitness forever. But the truth is, I didn't really start honing in on exercise and nutrition until the days of YourGymGF. And it's so important to note that I didn't make all of my lifestyle changes in one day. I started small, one substitution at a time.

I switched out processed wheat bread for organic sprouted grain bread. I cut my habit of grabbing a breakfast sandwich or muffin on my way to work and took the few extra minutes to whip up some egg whites, spinach and toast. I started using stevia instead of sugar. I limited myself to one scoop of ice cream instead of three. All of these small changes month by month and year by year added up to some pretty significant results.

With each positive step towards a "cleaner" nutritional routine, my sense of motivation, energy levels and happiness grew exponentially. My body literally began to change from the inside out. My complexion cleared up, and the spots of psoriasis on the back of my head went away.

After two years of dating Jack, I finally got him to jump on board too. He'd struggled since college with a severe form of seborrheic dermatitis that caused red, dry and painful inflammation on his face. He'd go down to the canal after shaving to splash some calming salt water on his face. Sometimes, when it got so bad, he couldn't even open his mouth to eat. It made him miserable and moody. Who wants to go out in public when your face looks and feels like it's on fire? I could never blame him.

I knew all along that nutrition played a major role in his skin condition, but at the time he wasn't ready to believe me. His dermatologist had long ago convinced him that this "condition" would never go away, and she insisted he use two topical creams she prescribed - the same creams that have multiple long-term side effects. This doctor pissed me off to no end because she wouldn't even entertain the possibility of an allergy or food having an effect on Jack's skin. I'd actually gone with Jack to an appointment to help him be more proactive, and she pretty much shot down all of my ideas without even pretending to consider them. Nice bedside manner. Thanks lady. Thanks for nothing, besides adding ineffective toxins to his daily routine.

It wasn't until Jack met a younger dermatologist while captaining a boat that he finally changed his mind. She'd mentioned trying whole foods and going gluten-free as the best way to manage his skin condition. It was absolutely life-changing. After just three days, he could already see decreased redness and inflammation. He was shocked to say the least. I can't say that I was.

Weeks later, he ditched the topical creams, and to this day doesn't use any prescription skin medication. He looks like a whole new Jack, and now knows without a doubt that nutrition plays a vital role in the overall health of his body…not just his weight. He also knows that if he drinks beer and eats shit all weekend, he's going to pay for it on Monday because it will flare his skin all over again. It's never as bad as it used to be since his diet has dramatically changed. However, he must remain aware of his triggers and how much of each he allows himself, to manage how he looks and feels.

I can't stress enough the importance of a healthy diet and the 80/20 lifestyle…and try like hell to stay away from the glyphosates (research if you aren't aware)! Do some reading in general on recent studies surrounding food and wellness; you really can't deny that happiness and overall well-being are directly affected by how you fuel your body and mind. And furthermore, if you have a skin condition, chronic pain, digestive problems etc., you need to realize that you have more control over these issues than you think. Be proactive. Find out what nutrients will best support your condition and what dietary triggers could be worsening it.

I recently had a nutrition evaluation – a blood and urine test measuring minerals, amino acids, digestive support and anti-oxidants. With the results, I was able to tailor a regimen to my own unique needs. I don't take any prescription medications, and I plan to hold off on doing so for as long as possible.

I realize there are certain illnesses and diseases that can benefit from prescription drugs, and I'm not advocating doing away with all modern medicine by any means. But if we can all invest some additional thought, time and energy into what we do (or don't) put into our bodies, it will only help us to live longer, healthier and happier lives. It's the only body you'll ever get. Isn't it worth it?

CHAPTER 19

THE CLIFF

Just because you jump doesn't mean you have to keep falling.

The sun beamed through the window and squinted my eyes open. I reached across the futon, clumsily slamming my hand around until it found my cell phone.

6:14am. It took all of two seconds for the awful gut feeling to resurface – the one that had begun the previous night, fueling my decision to sleep on this back-stabbing metal crate instead of nestled into my king size feathery cloud bed next to my husband. I'd only been married nine months. NINE MONTHS.

Luckily, all of my clothes were neatly organized in this spare room, thanks to the Cape style house with silly small closets that could probably fit a total of four winter coats if we were lucky. The once cozy home suddenly felt intensely suffocating in more ways than one.

I began filling my bright colored gym bag as my stomach swelled with murky waves and I choked on my own spit. This time I didn't just pack my usual Saturday morning fitness gear; I added some sundresses (the slinky ones that you can get away without ironing), a few more gym outfits and some other minimum essentials for a 21st century nomad woman - toothbrush, makeup bag and skin routine. I'd never packed like this before - sober, intentional packing. Far from a dumb alcohol-induced argument about our next vacation destination. One of the best (and worst) parts of my personality is that when I make a decision, it's non-negotiable. All chips are in. I wasn't coming back, and I knew it. My super sweet tenants to whom I'd rented for the past five years were about to get the "Thanks for the wedding gift, but I need my house back."

I tip toed down the stairs, doing my best not to disturb Jack or Maggie, our chocolate lab. Pausing at the door, I took in our rustic kitchen that I'm proud to say came out looking like something in Cape Cod HOME magazine once I was done with it. I caught Maggie peeking her head up from the living room dog bed to say her usual good morning. I wanted to cry, but no tears came. I swear her sweet puppy dog eyes were begging "Mummy don't go," although she was more likely just wondering how much time stood between her and breakfast.

Either way, it broke my heart. And I'm not even a dog lover. Well, I do love dogs…I just don't love them in my house. #sheddingkillsme. I crept towards her in stealth mode because she prefers little to no movement. Maggie really emBARKS on a relaxing lifestyle, if you will. I grabbed her face and kissed her keppie (my mom's Yiddish word for head).

6:42am. I started racking the squat bar with weights for my first set of leg day - the best and worst of all workouts combined into one. The dread of what lies ahead somehow always ends with endorphins flying through the ceiling and a hot start to the weekend. Plus, I give squats 75% of the credit for taking my "flattened with a spatula" ass to the next level of Bootytown, as mentioned in Chapter 1.

Looking back, I was completely focused on that leg routine as if it were any other day at the gym. Odd, considering I'd just made the decision to pack up and leave home with no goodbye or explanation. I also didn't care about Jack's family beach party starting at 9am. I wasn't going. I'd already made that decision too.

Just as I finished my first set, I noticed a scruffy bearded reflection in a backwards baseball cap coming my way. I could tell by his athletic build, broad shoulders and puffy chest strut that it was Mr. Buff! I hadn't seen him in years, and he was a refreshing familiar face on my old stomping grounds. This gym was about 30 minutes from "Jack's" house and right down the street from the house I'd proudly bought and lived in alone throughout most of my 20s. I'd met a lot of great people there, and Mr. Buff was one of them.

Before he knew it, I'd word vomited the last five years of my life, bringing him more than up to speed on my current rocky situation. Being a stand-up guy, he calmly listened, allowing me to talk his ear off. But I knew damn well that when I finished talking, I'd better be ready to hear some deep raspy feedback - his signature "ultimate advice," as I'd affectionately coined it.

Before I reveal Mr. Buff's life-changing advice, let me briefly address my relationship (although I think it's somewhat irrelevant at this point in my story). To be clear, Jack was and is a wonderful human being. Yes, he had faults like anyone else (including me). He made the typical relationship mistakes, like forgetting to switch the laundry over, but my restless disconnect was much more complex than that.

I felt guilty because Jack and his family were nothing short of amazing, supporting me throughout the most devastating experiences of my life. The only way I can find to remotely explain is that I felt lonely, disconnected and on a continuous search for deeper intimacy. The type of intimacy where your soul feels safe being naked and vulnerable. Intimacy so deep that you often can't physically see the person in front of you because the mental bond is far superior. Intimacy where age is just a number and your souls are forever young.   '

Even with Jack lying next to me in the quintessential Cape house, I went to bed every night lonely - stuck inside my head with so much to share, so much to say, so much to give and so much hope. Even with an abundance of solid relationships and countless life convos with friends and family, I somehow felt stuck in a cage. This little puppy needed to be let out of her crate!

So back to Mr. Buff. The words he spoke that day are still so clear in my mind...

"Ok Sarah...so you've climbed up this 'life' cliff for the past five years trying so hard to build what you want and following a cookie cutter method of how things should be done, right? You moved in with your boyfriend, got engaged a few years later and then got married…and you ignored some gut feelings and self-doubt along the way because you counted on things getting better. Correct? You're a hard worker, and that's what hard workers do. They don't throw in the towel. And then, in getting married, you took that big JUMP. You jumped right off that cliff and began to fall. But let me tell you something. Just because you've started to fall doesn't mean you have to keep falling. You're 33 years old, don't have any kids, are financially stable, have your own house and are a rock star" (Mr. Buff always called me a rock star, and I loved him for it).

"So, if you know in your gut that this isn't the right life path, put on your cape, your wings - whatever it is that makes you fly - and fly your ass back up! DO NOT continue to fall just because everyone around you is making you feel like that's what you're supposed to do. Having kids, buying a new house together - whatever it is you think might make it better - WON'T. You'll eventually fall too far, hit the water, start drowning and wonder how you got there. It's a hell of a lot harder to swim up from the bottom of the ocean to fly, so you'd better start considering that now. Sure, everyone will talk. People will be shocked, and social media gossip will fly for a month, but who gives a shit? You're the only person that needs to be happy with your life choices…not your friend of a friend of a friend in Tulsa who's miserable in her own marriage stalking your posts from halfway across the country."

For the next days, weeks and months, this unexpected philosophical conversation was burned into my brain. Mr. Buff's "cliff" perfectly conveyed how I was feeling, and to this day, it's one of my favorite analogies (and surprisingly simple if you think about it). I'm sure many of you will relate at some point in your life.

I want to make it clear that I don't believe in just giving up on marriage or any relationship for that matter. However, I wholeheartedly believe the foundation on which they're built need to be rock solid. And I guess in the end you're the only person who can determine if it is (or isn't) up to your standards. You can't go building a home to endure hurricanes on a half-ass foundation. If you do, you're only setting yourself up for devastation.

Hell, devastation can happen no matter how strong the foundation, but I'd much rather take my chances having the brick laid from the start. I want – no, I *need* the most durable structure that I can rely on for steady support - a substructure for my life, my hopes and my dreams. No one's going to huff and puff and blow my house down. But it was up to me to grow some wings and lay the groundwork (key word = WORK). This life shit ain't easy.

With that being said, I want to touch on social media, community and gossip because believe me, these were factors that even strong-willed Sarah considered when packing that gym bag. As someone who truly doesn't care if friends post a photo of me on the potty (I'm actually pretty sure they have...thanks Abby), I'll admit that I did care when it came to the perception of my relationship. Photos of Jack and me island hopping, going out to dinner three nights a week, dressing up our adorable pup and beaching it with family and friends pretty much took up all of Mr. Zuckerberg's Facebook storage. And it wasn't fake. We genuinely enjoyed our adventures, never fought and functioned pretty damn well maintaining a home together. So yes, I feared comments like, "Oh another couple who clearly pretended to have the perfect life on Fakebook," immediately followed by "he or she probably met someone else." The list of snide remarks my mind conjured up was endless.

But after my chat with Mr. Buff, I realized that at the end of the day, one person's idea of perfection can be very different than the next. And for me personally, some crucial deeper connection was just missing with Jack. Frankly, it's not the social media community's job (or right) to influence my life choices. My friend's sister-in-law does not and will never sleep next to me, spend time in my home, share a meal or help raise my children…for God's sake, she doesn't even have my phone number and pretends not to see me when I pass her in Target! But somehow, she's shocked that I'm getting divorced and judges me for making the "wrong" decision?!

Hmm. Funny because my closest friends who barely follow my social media know exactly what I feel, and they haven't questioned my thought process for one second. These friends will always be the people by my side on this roller coaster of life.

I'm not trying to make this realization sound easy. It was anything but. This "age of information" makes it extremely difficult to avoid getting caught up in what's being portrayed as reality vs. real life. It's scary and a little sad that when you choose to share your life and your soul with others, you become vulnerable to (often harsh) judgment. But I've found (and shown in earlier chapters) that there are a lot more people than you think who can emphasize with you. And at the end of the day if YOU are happy with your decisions and reality, then what can anyone else say?? You shouldn't have done that? You're an idiot for making yourself happy?

The best advice I can offer is to keep the priority of your own happiness at the center of all you do…and consider who will remain a part of your life 25 years from now. Who will still be there making life fabulously fulfilling? Those are the people who matter, but even they aren't the ones who have to wake up and live your life every day. Be selfish. Follow your gut. Do you. Strap on your wings and fly, even if you risk judgement from the trolls. If you follow this roadmap, you'll inevitably portray true happiness, giving others no choice but to be happy for you too!

CHAPTER 20

THE BUTTERFLY EFFECT

Life may seem like barreling full speed ahead into the unknown, but in reality, each seemingly insignificant movement can determine what lies ahead. Every choice we make in every moment holds the possibility of pushing open a door to endless opportunity and a real chance at finding what we truly need.

Who knew weekend road trips, frequent dinner dates and girl talk with my best friends could land me right where I needed to be in the romance department? Two months had passed since I'd packed up and left Jack's house, and for the first time in my life, I felt content. At peace. Suddenly without the resident anxious ticking of my heart running me around like a hamster on its wheel.

I felt terrific in my own skin. I was training hard at the gym and reviving my inner rock star with healthy nutrition (80% of the time, of course) and mindful mental nurturing. I wasn't obsessed with being skinny, funny, pretty, sweet or anything else that garners the affection of others. I felt strong. My confidence was back to being defined by me, and me only.

I'd already done 34 years of hard work – the soul-searching deliberation and process of elimination – inadvertently figuring out what I

DIDN'T want in a man to help me pinpoint the traits I sought in a lasting life partner…not that I was actively looking! But in addition to finding myself unexpectedly content, I couldn't help but notice that I was also left with a surprisingly clear picture of the type of guy I needed to find genuine happiness.

Naturally, after my divorce, my good friend Elle and I had numerous conversations over pizza and wine, "designing" my perfect match.

- What words would I use to describe this person?

- What personality traits would bring out the best in me?

- How exactly did I want to be treated?

- What were my non-negotiables when it came to certain behaviors? Will he go through his mail daily? (Well, he'll need to because I hate clutter…but I'm not ashamed…that's the real me.)

- What drives me? What are my deepest passions?

- What type of person could take the passenger seat as my teammate in life to help me achieve my goals?

Elle and I had chatted about all of this more times than I can count, but the right timing and means to my end still seemed so far off...so unattainable. For the first time in my life I knew exactly what I needed, but for the first time in my life I didn't have a clue how to get it. It wasn't as simple as grinding at a job search or sweating my ass off to build certain muscles.

Little did I know I was about to be taken on one hell of a ride! I was about to get pleasantly smacked in the face with an unexpected realization, learning firsthand what a fiery fuel self-assurance can be when it comes to meeting someone new. Apparently radiating that kind of energy acts like a magnet. It manifests a bizarre law of attraction. I guess it totally makes sense if you think about it. When you fill yourself up with the qualities, passion and love you seek, you attract others who align with your frequency.

I'dsoon find myself facing a life-altering choice. Should I lean into a bizarre chance encounter and roll with it at an irrational pace? Or should I play it smart, take a cautious step back and take my time? What the hell happens when you suddenly get handed everything you've ever asked for? Was I even ready to receive it? I was about to find out...

November 3, 2018. I met up with one of my besties, "Cass-doggie," for a night out in

Boston. She was in town working a business conference, and lucky for us, she was being put up at a five-star hotel in the Seaport District...my favorite. It's where all the young business professionals were bar-hopping, as opposed to where I lived in country bumpkinville 50 miles away.

We got all dolled up in the room together "college style," sipping on cocktails with pop music blaring as we pre-gamed for an exciting night ahead. But we weren't drinking $10 handles of Rubinoff or Burnett's raspberry vodka anymore. We were classy 30 somethings now. Our bodies weren't provocatively exposed. In fact, I remember Cass-doggie looking sophisticated as hell in her knee-length grey long sleeved dress, black tights and matching riding boots. Our conversations had also evolved from, "Who's having the late-night keg party?" to "Have you read 'You Are A Badass?'"

Like pretty much all of my girlfriends, Cass and I always have deep conversations, pleasantly interrupted by plenty of deep belly LOLs whenever we get together. I'm not sure if this is possible, but we may very well have known each other in another life. Maybe it's divine intervention or maybe it's just because we've been friends since way back in the tumultuous high school days …but we're both profoundly aware of the existence of some kind of innate connection. We're on the same wavelength in so many ways. We finish each other's sentences and seem to know what the other is thinking without saying a word. Which brings me to what came next…I'm holding Cass-doggie completely responsible for the fate of this carefree weekend on the town.

"Doggie, how's your Tindering going? Have you met anyone? Any good stories for me?" We're snuggled up in the king-size bed the following morning, both fighting dry mouth and cravings for greasy hangover food.

"Eh, nothing really worth reporting back, but you should totally get on there because it's super entertaining the first few days!"

And at that moment, on a lazy Sunday morning, something told me it would be a fabulous idea to make a first-time appearance on the social media dating gameshow.

I don't know about you, but I tend to think everything is ten times funnier after a night of drinking, especially my own dorky sense of humor. And suddenly there it was, tossed out to the world - a dating profile including four personal photos: a fitness photo shoot image, a cute red dress selfie, squat rack selfie, July 4th with friends and the absolute game changer…KERMIT. I included a photo of the loveable green Muppet on a scooter – a meme that read "My friends be getting into relationships and I be getting some more food….be right back". My only other self-description read, "Do you even deadlift?"

Looking back, my unconventional profile made perfect sense in finding a soulmate in this phase of life. I needed a guy who didn't take himself too seriously, had a passion for staying fit and possessed the unique combination of carefree open-mindedness and emotional depth that it takes to just "get" me.

At the risk of sounding like a conceited Tinder snob, I had several messages within minutes…

"You'll need to leave your job to travel the world with me." Yikes! Aggressive.

"Hi! How are you? How is your day going?" Boring as hell. I'd rather poke my own eyeballs out than chat with you, sir.

Overall, I found most of the men wayyy too eager to meet in-person, as in 10 minutes later. Love at first sight and random booty calls weren't what I was going for.

So, after a lot of laughs with Cass-doggie and almost puking from the hotel room's remnant scent of alcohol as I got dressed, I switched my Tinder profile off and headed home. There was no way I was allowing the local crowd to lay eyes on it.

Imagined future encounter with a hometown acquaintance: "Oh hey Sarah! I saw you on Tinder!"

"Um yeah, I saw you too, and I didn't swipe because we want nothing to do with each other."

Awkward, amiright?

The one exception made for re-activating my pun profile was to show a friend how the app worked later that afternoon. I had to give her the full experience.

If you're not familiar with Tinder, it basically prompts you to use a handful of photos and one short description to decide whether each featured candidate within a selected geographic radius is date-worthy.

Well, my friend got the full experience all right! Just as I switched my profile back on and began my finger swiping tutorial, a cute guy with a backwards Red Sox hat and genuine gleaming white, Grinch-sized smile popped up on my screen. You remember my irrational obsession with nice teeth from Chapter 1, don't you?

His description read "Looking for a fellow gym rat! I have zero expectations here. Let's see…I'm creative, love to cook, am an animal lover, work out, play hockey and travel. Love to be outside. Honest, very kind and loyal, almost to a fault. Love being with family and friends, watching sports and having thoughtful, deep conversations. I'm playful and love to laugh and have fun, and I am NOT looking for a hook-up."

Let's be honest. He had me at nice teeth and thoughtful deep conversations. And it certainly didn't hurt that one of his photos included his beach body – VERY nice to look at! Naturally I was swiping right on this one (which means I'm allowing the option to connect)! Why not??

And wouldn't you know, just as I swiped right, I was alerted that Grey had "super liked" me. For those of you happily matched, non-users, this is a big deal in the Tinder world. You're only allowed so many super likes. It's like those few bucks safely stored in your glove compartment for a Friday "make it to the weekend" coffee. It's not to be taken lightly.

And then BOOM. I had a private message waiting. Grey had written "Gym rat? You had me at deadlift," with a crying laughing emoji tacked on at the end. This was by far the most interesting prospect I'd come across in the last six hours, but I was itching to turn the app back off so locals couldn't spot me. After revealing a few quick facts about myself - working in the medical space, being fitness-orientated and thinking that online dating is an absolute shit show - we exchanged numbers. I had no idea this was the beginning of the end for me. Or should I say the beginning of so many new beginnings?

If you'd told me where I'd be now - a year after swiping right - I would have at the very least said you were full of shit. But this entire mind-blowing experience has once again shown me how fast life can fall apart just to fall right back into place for the better. It may come in hot, be completely unexpected and seem a little crazy, but I think often times our fear of the unknown is just anticipatory energy in our gut telling us something miraculous is right around the corner - the static hanging in the air before that storm's beautiful electricity is released.

But before I divulge where this electric current has led, I know you're dying to hear about the first few dates, right?

For starters, I cannot stress enough that I had no expectations...ZERO. I'm not sure that called for me showing up to meet him for the first time in gym clothes after a Monday night workout, but of course I did it anyway. Tight grey fitness capris, a black Under Armor long sleeved tee, with hair tossed up in a messy bun and my signature Lulu Lemon sweatband. I mean, I did go to the effort of touching up with a little bronzer and mascara, so I wasn't a total trash bag.

My theory with dating is "under promise and over deliver." Truthfully, I wanted to be sure Grey and I had some chemistry before showing him my cards. Just like all of those Tinder creeps dying to meet up mere minutes after seeing my photo, some men can get a little too overzealous if you put your sex appeal out there right away. At 33 years old, I wanted to be appreciated for my "raw" self. I wanted the attraction to be something more than "Hey, I want to rip your clothes off." Don't get me wrong, a sexual connection is crucial…but that's not what's going to keep a relationship going strong forty years from now.

So there I was, sitting in a booth at a sushi joint about 30 minutes from home, halfway between his place and mine. I was the only customer, and I felt it only appropriate that I celebrate my re-entry into the dating world with a glass of red wine. Neither of us had been to this restaurant before, but Google reviews said it was decent. I just wasn't quite sold on the ghost town dinner theme. The good news was I had a great view of the door, and my tunnel vision was fixed, eagerly anticipating my date's arrival.

It seemed like hours, but was probably more like a few minutes before Grey coolly sauntered in. There's no way in hell I could've missed him, standing 6 foot 4 inches tall at almost 250 pounds. He was definitely much taller than his Tinder photos suggested...and I was totally ok with that. I've always loved the idea of the stereotypically big, strong man who can envelop me. It makes me feel safe.

But more important than his stature, I was thrilled to see that Grey had also chosen gym clothes as his first date attire. He looked adorable and made me instantly comfortable with his down-to-earth vibe. And (sorry to be vein) I could see the separation of his shoulder muscles through his t-shirt. Yes, the chemistry was surely there.

After a quick introductory hug, he sat down across from me. It took his big body a little longer to slide into the booth, allowing me to take him in.

Apparently I was on a date with The Hulk, minus the green skin and short temper. He had a modest confidence about him, strong posture, broad shoulders, a proud chest and well-developed glutes that were hard to miss. I probably did a horrible job of convincing him I wasn't checking him out, but I didn't really care.

His soft hazel eyes were complimented by espresso hair like mine. It was short and clean-cut in an all-American style. His smile was broad like his shoulders, and he had a way of instantly putting me at ease. I hate to sound cliché, but it truly seemed like I had known him forever. I could tell he was calm and level-headed, and I quickly learned I could add great listener to the list. I mean, me being me, I really gave him no choice in the matter. He swears to this day I was nervous and chatty. I wasn't nervous, but I'll let him think so.

Nervous or not, we shared an eager exchange with enough mutual discussion for me to get his take on working out, nutrition, genetics and vaccines. Normal first date stuff, right? Although these arousing topics didn't lead to a goodnight kiss, they were enough to leave us both intrigued enough for another date.

Date #2. A Country Western bar on a Sunday night, almost a week later. We'd playfully harassed each other via text message all week long, and I was even more excited to see him again after catching a glimpse of the flirty sense of humor he'd somehow withheld on night one.

Enough of this mysterious shit! Ok fine, I'll admit it was kind of sexy.

Once again, I was at our meeting spot early to wait for him. I have an anxiety issue when it comes to being late. Thankfully, Grey walked in not long after I did, also early. More brownie points.

His voice was so raspy it was almost non-existent (from coaching earlier that evening, he explained). This somehow turned me on, along with his jeans and sneakers – the epitome of a hockey dad.

In contrast, I'd actually stepped it up a few notches with a hot LBD (little black dress), smoky eye makeup, hair down and a pair of high tan boots. But a sexy look didn't stop the dorky conversations from picking right back up where they'd left off.

Tonight's discussion focused on our 23andMe genetic reports, as he sipped his vodka soda and I some more red wine. Although talking through our ancestry phone screens may sound anything but erotic, this time our bodies were touching as we sat on bar stools pulled tightly together.

The conversation was already a lot flirtier than our sushi date. He had that gaze that looked right into my soul. I hated and loved that he didn't look away. He knew it too. Most people avoid direct eye contact as a result of inner insecurities…not Grey. He held that perfect threshold, making me blush without feeling at all threatened. I've always said there's a fine line between cocky and confident, and I wish more men knew this zone existed. Maybe Grey should write a book too because his effortless balance on that fine line landed him a first kiss in the parking lot as we said our goodbyes. I'll never understand how one of the most exhilarating feelings can be filled with nerves, excitement and nausea all at once. I'd so missed that feeling.

When I swiped right, and even in that moment of our first electric kiss, I didn't think it was possible that Grey could match my blueprint of the perfect partner…but I also wasn't about to discount this charming creature

the universe had dropped right in front of me.
So I didn't.

Date #3. Goes down as my favorite, which
will come as no surprise. I don't remember what
Grey made for dinner, I don't remember what
he was wearing and I don't remember the day of
the week.

My memory begins at the breakfast bar
as same-siders with our legs intertwined. I
didn't even get to finish whatever Phantom
Gourmet-worthy meal he'd prepared because
before I could take my next sip of wine, his bear
claws were deliberately but gently wrapped
around me, lifting me off my stool. Even at a
solid 135 pounds, I felt like a feather in his arms

as my fully flexed legs locked around his waist. He began softly kissing my lips, slowly inching his feet toward the bedroom. I found myself wondering if the urban legend of big feet was true…I'd find out soon enough.

Ut oh. This date was quickly sailing into unchartered waters as he cradled my neck and lay me down on the bed like a baby, sweeping a stray strand of hair out of my face to continue touching his lips to mine. I'd been dying for my own Fifty Shades episode, and I'd hit the jackpot.

The blood rushed through my body, and I could feel my face and throat getting hot. His hands made their way to the intersection of my bare goose bump skin and yoga pants. He peeled the stretchy fabric down my legs, covering them with still more kisses, one-by-one all the way to my toes. It was as if he'd spent years designing each deliberate kiss for the particular spot he caressed.

But this wasn't enough. I wanted him. I wanted all of his weight on top of me. And he wasn't giving in that easily. As he continued his methodical massage of my bare lower half, I gently interrupted him, rising to kneel on the bed with my hands held over my head, making it easy for him to slide off whatever was left. I was in the perfect position to do the same for him as he was now standing directly in front of me. And just like that, the eternal seconds spent waiting for this moment were over, and we connected simultaneously.

By now I was experiencing a shift in consciousness – a euphoric state that went well beyond sexual pleasure. I felt weightless. Nothing else mattered. Problems ceased to exist. I basked in the serenity of that moment, absorbing a feeling of utter completeness. I was physically exhausted and yet remarkably alive. How is it possible to experience this level of intimacy after just three dates?

That night somehow turned into a week-long stay at my house during the Holiday break when both of our offices shut down. So much for mysterious!

We almost broke up day one of his stay when Grey thought it would be cute to turn all of my spices, protein powder and supplements upside down in their cabinets. He convinced me that someday I'd smile seeing the Himalayan salt wrong side up. It's really annoying when he's right. I've come to find it endearing, as long as he goes no further in disrupting my organizational flow. It takes a lot longer than you'd think to get everything back in its proper place, and ain't nobody got time for that shit!

In all seriousness, it was incredible how easily he became in tune with my personality and all the quirks that make me tick, even innately knowing that I love a guy teasing me just the right amount.

Household pranks aside, the week was perfect…for us anyway. Each day began with a healthy breakfast made by Chef Grey, including all of my signature favorites - a veggie omelet, Ezekiel toast with peanut butter and sliced avocado. And breakfast is just the tip of the iceberg when it comes to his cooking A-game. Who said healthy foods can't be delicious? This guy needs his own #Fitman cookbook featuring all the effortless combinations he whips together…especially his sautéed chicken pesto with basil, sun dried tomato, capers and whatever the heck else he tosses in there. Almost as yummy as those glutes.

Sorry, back to breakfast...

We needed a well-rounded start to the day to fuel our shared gym sessions. Although typically a lone wolf in the workout department, I'm surprised at how much I enjoy workouts with Grey. Well, 90% of the time. On my tired, lazy days, the real Hulk comes out.

"I thought you had 225 on the squat rack last week. Is that 215?!"

I swear his day job is a coverup for some kind of private investigator/FBI shit he's got going because absolutely nothing sneaks by him. I sure got what I wished for (and then some) when I told Elle I was seeking an attentive teammate. Thank you, law of attraction, for your mystifying ways.

Our romantic fitness couple lifestyle didn't stop at the gym. We'd finish our morning routine with post-workout smoothies packed with berries, protein and whatever else was turned upside down in my cabinet. I'll even admit that our dorky chemistry proved to be even stronger when we realized we purchased several of the same brands for the same reasons.

By 2pm, it was time to shower and think about dinner because that's what foodies do. As you can tell, this Holiday week didn't consist of the most realistic adult life stressors. We were blissfully secluded on our own little cloud nine, focused on decisions like when to eat, how often to hit the gym, which cocktail to feature with dinner, and how much to indulge in our newfound snuggle addiction.

But don't chalk us up as a grotesquely mushy waste of space just yet! Another way in which Grey and I are frighteningly similar is that our curious little racing minds never quite shut off, even in the dreamy world of budding romance.

One of the many things Grey noticed during this initial bonding period was my skincare regimen. I make no bones about staying true to my routine, even in the presence of a new man…and especially not with one who shares my passion for clean, healthy products. I knew he'd be interested, if not a little turned on. Listen, don't you judge us just because organically manufactured goods get us excited! To each his own, right?

Within a day or two, Grey was firing off questions as to why I'd chosen certain ingredients and how they benefit my skin. I could tell he was impressed by my hassle-free organic regimen.

"Why don't you start your own skincare line? Your skin is beautiful and you're always glowing. It's the perfect time because more consumers than ever are concerned with toxins and trying to use cleaner products."

Yeah right. Just like that…start a skincare brand, huh? But his background in design and bringing products to market wouldn't allow me to brush off his suggestion as mere crazy talk. In his mind it made perfect sense, and he didn't let up. I didn't realize how serious he was until he started sending me mock-ups of logos and designs within days of our first skincare conversation.

And once again, I was faced with another law of attraction dilemma. I was terrified of the fire I saw in Grey because I also saw so much of myself. But this was exactly what I had wanted, wasn't it? A teammate and co-pilot - someone who wasn't scared to venture off and take chances with me.

And so, with less than two months of dating under our belts, Grey gave his design guidance to help me create a skincare brand, while I created the business entity and spearheaded the marketing initiative. Apparently with just the right combination of senseless passion and thoughtful energy, inconceivable things can magically come to life. Just months later, in April of 2018, ALOA Skincare (@aloaskincare) launched with a full website, social media and its first two products.

But that's not all that came to life...

One of my initial marketing efforts was to promote the Aloe Vera spray in the skin-cracking pool party climate of Las Vegas. Grey was traveling back from a business meeting in California, and had planned a stopover to meet his nephew there. We decided it was the perfect opportunity for me to fly out to meet him for a long Memorial Day weekend of business, mixed with plenty of pleasure.

Ladies and gentlemen, I'm living proof that what happens in in Vegas doesn't always stay in Vegas! A few weeks after our trip, I discovered I was pregnant. And so, our journey together began - taking chances on gut feelings, undeniable chemistry, crazy ideas and the excitement of a baby on the way.

Although this was not planned, I've never been happier. Everything about Grey coming into my life was completely unexpected, and I'm sure people looking in from the outside have wondered what the hell I was doing. For God's sake, even I was wondering what the hell I was doing at times! But in the end, life isn't always about sense and logic.

The fact is that each time I was faced with an unexpected choice, I did what felt right in my gut and my heart, somehow trying to follow a path that had no definitive conclusion. And I'm so thankful I ignored that little voice of logic, questioning whether this was the smart or popular path because my "senseless" decisions were, in the end, the sequential actions that have miraculously blossomed into some of the most fulfilling days of my life.

Before I met Grey, I didn't realize how truly powerful our energy and actions can be in propelling us in auspicious directions without even realizing it's happening. And I think that's how the things that are meant to happen do…without you even realizing that one flap of a butterfly's wings could possibly be influencing a storm's winds halfway around the world, days from now. I firmly believe that all of our individual vibrations and choices push us towards the better (or worse) days ahead. What if I had listened to that doubt in my head telling me that Tinder was just a silly dating app? What if I hadn't taken the chance of meeting Grey in that sushi bar? What if I had laughed off Grey's idea of a skincare line? We would have missed out on all of the joy and successes we've found.

And we're just getting started! Who knows what Grey and I can accomplish together from here? I know that building our life together and raising our son will be anything but easy...but I'm so invigorated by the bond and passion we share that I look forward to facing these challenges together. I can't wait to see what greatness today's choices will spur for our future. The possibilities are endless, and we never would have had the opportunity to reach them if we had tried to slow down the chaotic unknown that helped bring us together.

CHAPTER 21

FELLOW DIGGERS

Be picky with those allowed in your circle. The right tribe builds a positive lifestyle and a more fruitful path...kind of a no-brainer!

I've said it before and I'll say it again. I love to watch a Sunday football game and crush a plate of nachos with extra guacamole. But I also love waking up early Monday morning with a mission to be successful for the week - a mission to feel positive about myself and what I'm contributing to this world. It's a kind of high to wake up feeling refreshed - eager to jump out of bed and be productive. I like to think of it as making each day my bitch.

My lifestyle choices are critical to sustaining this mantra. There's no way in hell you'll find me sitting at an after-work cocktail hour every day, sipping on a sugary mixed drink, munching on a greasy pepperoni pizza, perpetuating the latest nasty rumors flying. There will always be those special occasions where I relax, celebrate and indulge, but it will never become routine. And I will always hold myself accountable for my thoughts, words and actions – ensuring that they only contribute to positivity and personal growth. I focus on living my best life - bettering myself and those that I love, instead of wasting energy on gluttonous, petty or negative indulgences.

Instead, you'll find me in the gym taking a boxing class, in my kitchen meal prepping for the week or fundraising for a cause that inspires me. It's only logical that I associate myself with those who show this same dedication. A typical weeknight out with girlfriends includes taking a boot camp workout class before catching up over sushi.

My girls are no doubt the "work hard, play hard" kind of crew. All of them, in their own way, elevate my standards for the kind of life I choose, whether it means pushing me to finish a grueling workout or playfully poking fun of shitty grammar in my social media post.

It also means that the women I call my best friends support my personal choices and priorities…even if theirs don't perfectly align with mine…even if they don't fully understand the motives behind mine. I didn't doubt for one second that my true friends would stick by me when I made the decision to leave Jack. And I knew without ever glancing back that they were in my corner, offering any support possible as I grappled with the choice to follow my heart to Grey, the business and our baby.

Although we're all born with a genetic predisposition for certain traits, there's no doubt we're also very much a product of the community and lifestyle we hand-pick. The ability to surround yourself with people and circumstances whose raw energy lifts you up is one of the most important life skills. It's likely not something you'll develop in childhood, and you'll probably make more than a few wrong choices along the way. But if you can find that wonderful balance of a strong mental compass, steering you towards those who inspire challenge and growth, you'll reap inconceivable benefits.

My closest friends made over the years bring with them quite diverse personalities; they all offer a different angle, helping me from my own definitive perspective. They've taught me that by being vulnerable and not judging, we have a lot more in common than we may have initially thought. When you make the effort to see the best in others, they'll see the best in you.

I make the conscious decision daily to associate myself with these cultivating souls who bring out the best version of me - family and friends who challenge me to continually improve myself in relationships, intelligence, creativity, health, fitness, work, play and everything in between. There's a good chance my "people" don't even realize the extent of their contributions to my vitality, but I want it known that it's those around me - supporting me through the tragedy, merriment and mundane - who have molded me into the woman I'm proud

to be. I'm honored to have them in my corner –
my fellow diggers for life's deeper meaning. I
didn't have the idea to write this book…my
friends did. And they pushed me to make it
happen.

Author's Note

We all have a life path. How much we can or cannot control we'll probably never know. What we do know for certain is that we make a conscious choice each day in how we receive this life and all of its trauma, beauty, heartache and joy. We choose our attitude. We choose to love or hate. We choose to embrace or reject. We choose to sit on the pity pot or cherish the value.

My choice, just as my brother encouraged before leaving this world, is amor fati - to love thy fate - because it's pretty damn beautiful that I'm the only human to ever live this life and walk this particular path, just as you're the only one to walk yours.

Whenever you find yourself less than confident, self-loathing, wishing you were more like someone else, take a step back and think just how miraculously unique it is to be YOU. Remind yourself that you're the only one guaranteed to spend the rest of your life with you. So soak up the lessons life offers and never stop striving for your best self. Choose to live the rest of your life in the company of a rockstar.

I would like to give special thanks to Chelsea Roy, one of my best friends and editor of Love Thy Fate. She is one of the most talented people I know, and if not for her I would not be publishing this book. Thank you for your inspiration and guidance, Chels!

Chelsea Roy is a freelance writer based on Cape Cod, MA. Born with infectious energy, a collaborative spirit and a passion for playing with words, her childhood short stories, poetry and editing of classmates' homework assignments evolved into a Bachelor of Arts degree in English from Providence College, experience in public relations, marketing, blogging, social media and book editing.

Chelsea delivers tailored written content and strategy solutions across a variety of industries, independent professionals and authors looking to build their brand and tell their stories. She can be contacted at her website here: **www.chelsearoycontentcreation.com**

34018493R00196

Made in the USA
Middletown, DE
21 January 2019